W9-ATY-983

UNIX®
Quick Reference

Que Quick Reference Series

Ben Hunsburger

with introductory material by Ralph Roberts

UNIX Quick Reference

Copyright © 1994 by Que® Corporation

Library of Congress Catalog No.: 94-65878

ISBN: 1-56529-770-9

96   95   94   4   3   2   1

Interpretation of the printing code: the rightmost double-digit
number is the year of the book's printing; the rightmost single-digit
number, the number of the book's printing. For example, a printing
code of 94-1 shows that the first printing of the book occurred in
1994.

Publisher
David P. Ewing

Associate Publisher
Michael Miller

Publishing Director
Joseph B. Wikert

Publishing Manager
Brad R. Koch

Acquisitions Editor
Angela J. Lee

Acquisitions Coordinator
Patricia J. Brooks

Product Director
Robin Drake

Production Editor
Linda Seifert

Copy Editor
Danielle Bird

Technical Editor
Steve Pryor

Book Designers
Amy Peppler-Adams
Paula Carroll

Cover Designer
Amy Peppler-Adams

Production Team
Angela Bannan, Greg Eldred, Brook Farling, Bob LaRoche,
Joy Dean Lee, G. Alan Palmore, Nanci Sears Perry,
Linda Quigley

Composed in *Stone* and *MCPdigital* by Que Corporation.

Table of Contents

Appendix—Regular Expressions   291

Index   297

Introduction

UNIX Quick Reference is a quick guide to the rich range of commands on a UNIX system. While general in scope, this book covers the essential commands available on most UNIX systems. Specific flavors of UNIX supported include UnixWare, SCO UNIX, Solaris, AT&T UNIX, XENIX, and many others. While small differences in names or usage of commands may occasionally pop up, you will find the command information generic enough to serve most uses.

UNIX Quick Reference isn't intended to replace comprehensive documentation. The book is more like an abridged dictionary of common commands. You can find more detailed information about UNIX in one of Que's other UNIX books. Beginning and intermediate users can learn all the basics with *Introduction to UNIX*, Second Edition. If you just need a quick refresher, want to learn only a few specific facets of UNIX, or prefer to read books with a light, humorous style, consult *I Hate UNIX!* For in-depth coverage of all facets of UNIX, *Using UNIX*, Special Edition is a good choice. All of these books are good additions to your computer library.

Organization of This Book

The opening section of this book, the Task Listing, provides a list of commands grouped according to general function. For example, commands used in archiving are referenced together, as are those for editing. In UNIX, tasks often can be accomplished in several ways—seeing all related commands together should help you to find and compare the commands and then find the most efficient command for a specific job.

Within the Command Reference section, commands are presented alphabetically. Each command's purpose and syntax are provided; *syntax* is the information typed along with the command's name for a specific result. Additional information for each command may include notes, cautions, examples of usage, rules for using the command, and so on.

> **Note**
>
> UNIX is case-sensitive. Various commands are interpreted differently depending on whether they are typed in upper- or lowercase. Use the commands in this book exactly as they are shown.
>
> Keep in mind that you must press the Enter or Return key after typing a command to execute the command.

The final section of this book, the Appendix, provides detailed instructions on using regular expressions with UNIX commands such as `grep`, `egrep`, `more` and so on.

Conventions

Certain conventions are used in this book to help you understand the commands more easily. The following table describes these conventions.

Format	Description
`special font`	This format is used for UNIX commands, options, names of files and directories, and system output, such as prompts and messages.
`bold special font`	This format shows user input, such as commands, command options, and names of directories and files used as arguments.
`italic special font`	This font shows the names of variable elements to which values are given by the user, such as *filename* or *increment*.

Task List

This task list can help you find a command to perform a certain kind of task. Every effort has been made to organize these commands into meaningful categories.

Task	Description
Archiving	Place files on removable media, or compress files. Typically for long-term storage.
Comparing	Compare directories and files.
DOS	Used for DOS-compatible media.
Editing	Work with the UNIX editors.
File Information	Report information about files.
File Manipulation	Location of stored files and how the files are treated in the directory.
File Processing	Read files and produce output from them in modified form.
File Viewing	View the contents of the files with varying viewing control.
Miscellaneous	These commands don't fit into any major category.
Office and Desktop Utilities	Useful utilities for the office and desktop.
Printing	Print files and use printers.
Process Scheduling	Schedule jobs to be executed at certain times.

(continues)

Task	Description
Screen Handling	Affect the status of the screen you are working on.
Scripting	Useful when writing shell scripts.
Searching	Search the contents of files and the file system for file names.
Serial Communication	Provide you with serial communication capabilities with other machines.
System Information	General information about the system, disk utilization, current working environment, hardware configuration.
System Maintenance	Used in general system maintenance.
User Information	Provide information about users on the system.
User Maintenance	Allow you to manipulate user-oriented information.

Archiving

Command	Description
cpio	Makes backups, including the UNIX special files.
format	Formats floppy disks.
pack, pcat	Compress files.
unpack	Uncompresses files.
compress, uncompress, zcat	Compresses/uncompresses files.

Command	Description
dd	Allows you to write to devices without using structure.
diskcp	Copies the contents of a floppy disk.
dtype	Reports the type of media written on a floppy disk.
pcpio	Portable cpio.
ptar	Portable tar.
tar	Makes backups (tape archive).

Comparing

Command	Description
diff	Compares two files and reports what must be done to one to make it look like the other.
dircmp	Compares two directories, reporting the files unique to each directory. If the same name is used dircmp reports if the files have the same contents or not.
bdiff	Allows you to run a diff process on files too large for diff command.
cmp	Does a byte-by-byte comparison of two files.
comm	Finds the lines that are common between two sorted files. Three columns are generated: the lines found only in the first file, those only found in the second file, and the lines found in both files.

(continues)

Command	Description
diff3	Similar to diff but used for three files at a time.
diskcmp	Compares two floppy disks using cmp. (see diskcp).
sdiff	Runs diff with the results shown side by side.

DOS

Command	Description
doscat	Reads a DOS diskette and runs cat on a file on that disk.
doscp	Copies files back and forth between DOS disks and UNIX.
dosdir	Mimics the DOS DIR command on the DOS disk.
dosformat	Formats a disk for DOS.
dosls	Performs the UNIX ls command on a DOS disk.
dosrm	Performs the UNIX rm command on a DOS disk.
dosmkdir	Makes a directory on the DOS disk.
dosrmdir	Removes a directory from the DOS disk.
dtox	Strips the carriage return character and the end-of-file marker (^Z) from files.
xtod	Adds the carriage return character when a new line is encountered.

Editing

Command	Description
ed	A line editor.
vi	A full-screen editor that uses ed commands.

File Information

Command	Description
l	Gives a detailed (long) directory listing.
lc	Produces a columnar directory listing.
ls	Lists the files found in the file system.
wc	Counts the bytes, words, and lines in a file.

File Manipulation

Command	Description
copy	Copies files and directory structures.
chmod	Allows you to change the permissions of a file.
rm	Removes files (deletes them).
umask	Allows you to set default permissions for file creation.
chown	Allows you to change the owner of the file.

(continues)

Command	Description
cd	Allows you to change your working directory.
cp	Copies files.
chgrp	Allows you to change the group owner of the file.
ln	Allows you to create links (or aliases) for files.
mkdir	Makes a directory.
mv	Renames a file (moves it).
rmdir	Removes a directory.
touch	Allows you to change the access and modification times of a file, or to create a new file with specific times.

File Processing

Command	Description
cat	Concatenates files.
cut	Extracts fields from a list of files.
join	Extracts the common lines from two sorted files.
nl	Adds line numbers to files.
paste	Produces columnar output from one or more files, where each file contributes a column of the output. paste is often used with cut to reorder columns in a file.
pr	Processes files and writes them to the standard output after applying formatting.

Command	Description
sort	Sorts text files based on user definable keys.
split	Divides a file into defined chunks.
tr	Translates/maps the input of a file from one set of matched characters to a new set.
uniq	Strips repeated lines from a sorted file based on a specified key value.

File Viewing

Command	Description
cat	Displays the contents of a file on-screen.
head	Shows the first several lines of a file.
more	Allows you to view lines of a file one page or screen at a time and search for text in that file.
pg	Same as more but also allows you to go backward in the file.
pr	Processes files and writes them to the standard output after applying formatting.
tail	Shows the last several lines of a file.
tee	Takes the input from a pipeline and allows you to split that output. A copy goes to a file and a copy continues down the pipeline.
hd	Shows you the contents of files as hexadecimal numbers; a hex dump.

(continues)

Command	Description
nl	Adds line numbers to files.
od	Shows you the contents of files as octal numbers; an octal dump.

Miscellaneous

Command	Description
banner	Produces an "enlarged" version of the arguments passed it.
write	Allows you to pass messages to a user on his or her screen.
crypt	Encodes a file for security purposes.
hello	Allows you to pass a message to a user on his or her screen. Similar to write.
mesg	Controls whether a user can write messages to your terminal.

Office and Desktop Utilities

Command	Description
bc	A calculator.
cal	Produces a calendar.
mail	Allows for electronic mail.
calendar	Searches for scheduled events to mail you. Invokes a reminder service.
checkmail	Checks on the status of mail you have tried to send.

Command	Description
dc	Another calculator (not as intuitive as bc).
news	Checks for the presence of systemwide news.
spell	Checks spelling of a text file.

Printing

Command	Description
cancel	Cancels a print job.
disable	Disables a printer; doesn't allow the queued jobs to print.
enable	Enables a printer; allows the queued jobs to print on the printer.
lp	Queues the request for something to be printed.
lpstat	Checks the status of the system printers and print jobs.
lprint	Prints files locally to printers attached to terminals.

Process Scheduling

Command	Description
at / batch	Schedules a job to run at a later time, or when system resources are more suitable.

(continues)

Command	Description
cron	Manages when scheduled jobs are run.
crontab	Submits jobs to run on a routine basis to cron.
nice	Allows you to run jobs in the background at a different priority.

Screen Handling

Command	Description
clear	Clears the screen.
tabs	Sets tab stops on a terminal.
setcolor	Sets the color palette of an ANSI terminal.

Scripting

Command	Description
csh	The C shell.
echo	Takes the named arguments and writes them to standard output.
line	Reads a line of input from the standard input.
logname	Reports under what user name you logged in originally.
sh	The Bourne shell.
sleep	Stops executing for a defined number of seconds.

Command	Description
tee	Takes the standard input, redirects that to a file, and passes it on as standard output.
test	Allows you to test whether a set of criteria are true.
true	Always returns a zero exit status (used in looping continuously).
awk	A programming language to manipulate text files, typically for creating reports from these text files.
basename	Returns the file name portion of a path name; it strips the directory name.
dirname	Opposite of basename; it returns the directory portion of the path name.
expr	Allows you to evaluate expressions in shell scripts. These expressions can be mathematical, or string oriented. String functions include returning substrings, length of a string, and more.
yes	Always returns a "y" character, useful if you want to force a positive response to a "yes/no" prompt.

Searching

Command	Description
what	Searches files for the occurrence of the character sequence @(#), and prints the characters that follow; used in SCCS (source code control system).

(continues)

Command	Description
find	Looks for file names that match a certain criteria (name, file size, modification time, and so on).
grep, egrep, fgrep	Searches the contents of files for the text and patterns passed them.
strings	Looks for printable character strings in binary files.

Serial Communications

Command	Description
cu	Allows you to connect to another computer and log in as if you were a terminal at the local site.
uucp	Allows you to copy files from one machine to another. uucp is a file transfer program.

System Information

Command	Description
date	Displays the system date and also can be used to set the system date.
devnm	Reports the name of the device where the mounted file system is stored.
df	Reports free space on the file system.
du	Reports the space usage for the list of directories given it.

Command	Description
env	Reports the current environment variables that have been exported.
file	Gives a good estimate as to the nature of the file given as an argument.
ps	Queries the status of processes in the job queue.
pwd	Reports the present working directory.
time	Shows how long something took to run.
tty	Reports the device name of the terminal you are currently logged onto.
uname	Reports information on the system, such as node name and the release of the operating system.
hwconfig	Shows a listing of the hardware configured on the machine.
last	Reads from the /etc./wtmp file and reports the history of logins and logouts from the system.
swconfig	Reports on the software installed on the system.
w	Reports who is logged on the system and what they are doing. It also reports how many users are on the system, how long the system has been up, and the load averages.

System Maintenance

Command	Description
kill	Allows you to kill (send signals to) processes.
shutdown	Shuts down the system.
stty	Reports and changes the control settings on ports.
sync	Forces the write behind buffers to be written to the disk.
wall	Sends a message to all of the currently logged on users.
assign / deassign	Allows you to control access to the floppy drives in a secure environment.
mknod	Adds device name "hooks" to kernel device drivers.
mnt, umnt	Mounts and unmounts file systems.

User Information

Command	Description
id	Reports your current user identification.
logname	Reports how you originally logged onto the system.
w	Reports who is logged onto the system and what they are currently running.
who	Reports who is logged onto the system.

Command	Description
whodo	Reports who is logged onto the system and what they are currently running.
finger	Allows you to display information about users on the system.

User Maintenance

Command	Description
newgrp	Allows you to change your working group.
passwd	Allows you to change your password.
su	Allows you to become another user (substitute).

Command Reference

This command reference is provided as a means of covering some of the more common commands you may use in the UNIX environment. This is not meant to be an exhaustive listing. After the command is listed, it is described as to what function it fulfills or why you would want to use the command. Following this is a syntax line. The syntax line shows what "format" you have to use to type in the command. For example:

```
cp source dest
```

In this example cp is the command; *source* and *dest* are arguments.

When parts of the command are enclosed in square brackets [ ], it means that the enclosed text is optional and does not have to be supplied for the command to do something. Words in the syntax in italics are descriptions of arguments you need to supply. After the syntax, is a detailed description of what each element of the command means and its effect on the command. A notes section is provided to explain various facets of the command and things to look out for, or basic premises needed to be done. A messages section is provided to show you what would happen if the command was misused and what those messages. This is followed by the examples section that demonstrates how to use the command in some real-world situations. Finally, the examples section is followed by a cross-reference of related commands.

assign

assign designates a device to a particular user and restricts access to other users. On many systems the devices are publicly accessible, and such assignments are not necessary. On security conscience systems, device assignment can enhance the level of security for users who work with sensitive data.

Syntax

```
assign [flags] device

deassign [flags] device
```

Argument or Option	Description
device	The name of the assigned device.

Flags

Argument or Option	Description
-d	Duplicates the action of deassign.
-v	Displays the devices that are assigned or unassigned.
-u	Performs error-checking; no assignment is made.

Rules

The user who wants to be assigned the device is the user who invokes the command. In a sense, the command is misnamed because no one assigns anything; a user must request the device assignment.

The system-defined user, asg, owns all assignable devices. On the first invocation of assign, the operating system builds the file /etc/atab. This file contains a list of assignable devices and designated users.

To add a device to the list of assignable devices, simply make asg the owner of the device. To remove a device from the list, make the owner something other than asg, for example, bin. To activate these changes, deassign all devices, delete the /etc/atab file, and reassign the devices.

A *raw device* acts as a blank sheet of paper so that you can provide your structure or none at all. The raw device is automatically assigned and may not be asked for separately. An error message is produced if you try to request the raw device separately.

Message

```
can't assign device
```

The device isn't in the assignable device table or you requested the assignment of a raw device.

Examples

```
assign fd096
```

Command assigns the current user the raw floppy disk and the block device.

```
deassign fd096
```

The user relinquishes device ownership.

at

Schedules jobs to execute at a later time. batch runs the command with a lower priority at a point when system utilization is lower—it may run immediately and it may run later, depending on the system load.

Syntax

```
at -qqueue time

at -l job-ids

at -r job-ids

batch
```

Argument or Option	Description
-qqueue	An optional queue designation may be specified. queue may be any letter between a and z, and the queue is defined as discussed under queuedefs(F) in the manual page. a is the default.
time	This is the time when the job starts. The format of time is highly flexible, and is divided into three basic parts: time, date, and increment.

<table>
<tr><td></td><td>time</td><td>This may be 1, 2, or 4 digits. If 1 or 2 digits are used, this is interpreted as hours. (at 1, at 10). If 4 digits are used, this means hours and minutes; a colon also may be used (at 0815, or at 8:15). The suffix am and pm may be used, otherwise a 24-hour clock is assumed. noon, midnight, and now also are acceptable.</td></tr>
<tr><td></td><td>date</td><td>This can be a month name followed by a day number and an optional year number preceded by a comma:

```
at 9:00am Dec 25
at 9:00 Dec 25, 1992
```

It also can be a day spelled out or abbreviated:

```
at 9:00 Friday
at 9:00 Fri
```

Special days are today and tomorrow. today is the default.</td></tr>
</table>

Argument or Option	Description
increment	Enables you to state an increment of the given time/date as +*n* units. Units may be *minutes*, *hours*, *days*, *weeks*, *months*, or *years*. The singular also is acceptable. *next* may be used to mean the same as +1.
-l *job-ids*	Lists the currently scheduled jobs. The list may be limited to specific job ids. When no *job-id* is specified all jobs are listed. If you are not the super user, then only your jobs are listed.
-r *job-ids*	Removes the specified *job ids* from the queue. Unless you are the super user, you may only remove your own jobs.

Notes

at takes all of its commands from standard input. Therefore, the commands are piped to it, redirected to it, or entered interactively.

at returns a job id when it is invoked. This id may then be used as the *job-id*(s) parameter described previously.

Only those users specified in the file /usr/lib/cron/at.allow are allowed to schedule jobs. If this file doesn't exist, then the file /usr/lib/cron/at.deny holds the list of users who can't use at.

If the time specified is less than the current time then the next occurrence of the time is used. For example, if at noon is used and it is 1:00 p.m. then the next day is used.

The standard output and standard error of the commands executed are mailed to the user via UNIX e-mail.

Message

```
at: bad date specification
```

You have entered a time for the execution to take place that is not formatted properly.

Examples

```
at noon <doit
```

Runs the commands found in the file doit at noon.

```
at noon Wed next week <doit
```

Runs the commands at noon on Wednesday of next week.

```
at 8:00 Dec 15 <mail-cards
```

Here is the file mail-cards that contains a list of commands to mail some electronic Christmas cards.

```
batch
date
find / -name "*.old" -print
```

This is an example of interactively entering commands to be executed by batch. To end this list of commands, type Ctrl-d. at may be used interactively as well. In this example, you are going to batch a search for files ending with the characters .old.

See also

cron, date, find, mail

awk

awk, a very powerful scripting programming language, is useful when generating reports from text based files. awk supplements the file processing capabilities of the shells: sh, csh, and ksh. You can process files based on pattern matches of certain fields. awk also gives you C-like structured programming constructs, and a printf command much like that of C. These capabilities allow for fairly straightforward programming and robust formatting of output.

The power of awk is beyond the scope of this discussion. Several good books are available on awk programming.

Syntax

```
awk [ -Ffldsep ] [ [-e] '¦" awk_code '¦" ] ...\
[ -f  awk_code_filename ] ... [ [ -v ] var=init_val
➡... ] [ filelist ]
```

Flags

Argument or Option	Description
-Ffldsep	An optional field separator. fldsep may be a regular expression, a single character, or a t to mean the tab character. The default field separator is white space (spaces and tab characters). The awk variable FS may also be used to control the field separator in the awk code.
-e '¦"awk_code '¦"	An optional script of awk code. The awk_code is the actual script to run. It may be enclosed in either single (') or double (") quotation marks. Use one or the other depending on how you want the shell (sh) to interpret the awk_code. Single quotation marks do not allow shell interpretation. Double quotation marks allow you to pass shell environment variables to the scripts. The -e is optional. You may chain several of these

(continues)

Argument or Option	Description
	awk_code instances on the command line. Each instance is appended to the last and executed as the complete program.
-f *awk_code_filename*	An optional file name holding awk code. You may specify several of these on the command line. The contents of the files are concatenated and executed as the complete program.
-v *var=init_val*	Allows you to specify an initial value for a variable used in your awk code. You may specify several values on the command line.
filelist	An optional list of files for the awk script (program) to manipulate. If no file is specified, awk assumes its input is the standard input.

Rules

Awk code has this general form:

    pattern   { *action* }

This form may be repeated several times. That is, you may have more than one pattern   { action } combination.

Argument or Option	Description
pattern	This is the pattern to match. Awk reads each record of the input file list and compares it to the pattern specified here. If no pattern is specified the associated action is always performed. Two special patterns are BEGIN and END. BEGIN is executed once on script entry, and END is executed just before script exits. Patterns may be any valid regular expression.

Argument or Option	Description
Regular expressions	
/expr/	Scans the current record for the expression's *expr*. If a match is found, the associated action is performed.
expr	Tests the expression *expr*. If the expression is true, the associated action is performed.
expr1 && expr2	Both expressions *expr1* and *expr2* must be true for the associated action to be performed.
expr1 || expr2	If either expression *expr1* or *expr2* is true, the associated action is performed.
(expr)	Allows for grouping of expressions.
!expr	Negates the expression such that if the expression is not true, the associated action is performed.
beg_expr, end_expr	Matches all records between the first expression *beg_expr* and the last expression *end_expr*.
Operators	
<	Less than
<=	Less than or equal to
>	Greater than
>=	Greater than or equal to
==	Equal to
!=	Not equal to.

(continues)

Argument or Option	Description
{ *action* }	This is the action performed when the pattern is matched. Each action block must be enclosed in curly braces. Each action statement is terminated with a semicolon (;). Action statements may consist of built-in functions, flow control statements (if, while, do, and for), input functions, and output statements.

Flow control

while (*test_expr*) *statement*

As long as the expression *test_expr* is true, *statement* is executed.

if (*test_expr*) *statement1* [else *statement2*]

The expression *test_expr* is tested, if true *statement1* is executed, otherwise if the optional else clause is present, *statement2* is executed.

for (*init_expr* ; *test_expr* ; *increment_expr*) *statement*

On entry to the for loop, the expression *init_expr* is evaluated. This expression is only evaluated once in the for loop. The expression *test_expr* is evaluated then, and if true *statement* is executed. After *statement* is executed, the expression *increment_expr* is evaluated, and the expression *test_expr* is evaluated. If *test_expr* is true than the process starts over.

do *statement* while (*test_expr*)

This is like the while statement, except that *statement* is executed at least once before the expression *test_expr* is evaluated.

Argument or Option	Description
break	Used with the looping flow control statements: for, while, and do. break is a controlled "go to" statement. It allows you to force the looping to stop as if the *test_expr* were no longer true, and execution continues.
continue	Used with the looping flow control statements: for, while, and do. continue is a controlled "go to" statement. It allows you to stop processing the current iteration of the loop and return control to the beginning of the loop.
next	Causes the next input record to be read and control is passed back to the first *pattern* statement of the entire script.
exit	Causes execution to go straight to the END statement. If no END statement is present, execution is halted.

Operators (in order of precedence)

$	Field indicator ($1 means field one, $2 means field two, $*n* means field *n*, $0 means the whole record)
++ --	Increment and decrement
^	Exponential
!	Logical negation
+ -	Unary plus and unary minus
* / %	Multiply, divide, and modulo
+ -	Addition and subtraction

(continues)

Argument or Option	Description
(no op)	No operation specified is an implied concatenation of strings. Strings are concatenated simply by juxtaposition.
< <= > >= != ==	Logical relations (less than, less than or equal to, greater than, greater than or equal to, not equal to, and equals, respectively)
~ !~	Regular expression match, negated regular expression match.
in	Array membership
&&	Logical and
||	Logical or
? :	Conditional expression
= += -= *= /= %= ^=	Assignment (equals, add to and set equals, subtract from and set equals, multiply by and set equals, divide by and set equals, modulo and set equals, and raise to the power of and set equals, respectively). These are borrowed from the C programming language.

The conditional expression

```
test_expr ? true_expr : false_expr
```

The expression *test_expr* is evaluated. If it is non-empty and non-zero, then the expression *true_expr* is executed, otherwise the expression *false_expr* is executed.

Argument or Option	Description

Output

print *expr1* , *expr2* , ..., *expr(n)*

print prints the arguments (expressions) given. Each placement of a comma (,) indicates where print places the output field separator. The end of the record is written with the record separator. When commas are omitted they are concatenated and assumed to be the same field. Assuming an output field separator of a colon (:), consider the following two examples.

print hello, how, are, you,? hello:how:are:you:?

print hello how, are you? hello how:are you?

---

printf (*format* , *expr1* , *expr2* , ..., *expr(n)*)

printf in awk follows the same rules as the printf(S) routine in the C programming language. Where print assumed the output field and record separators, printf prints how it is formatted based on the format, *format*. *format* consisting of a string specifying where numbers, strings, hard coded text and special strings should go.

Valid format operators are:

%c   A character

%d   A decimal integer

%e   Scientific notation in the form of [-]*d*.*dddddd*E[+-]*dd*

(continues)

Argument or Option	Description
%f	Scientific notation in the form of [-]*ddd*.*dddddd*
%g	The shorter of %e or %f
%o	An unsigned octal number
%s	A string
%x	An unsigned hexadecimal number
%%	An actual percent sign
\n	A newline
\b	A backspace
\f	A form-feed
\r	A carriage return
\t	A tab
ddd	An octal value of *ddd*

Variables

awk allows you to define your own variables. Notice from the operators table that fields are designated using the dollar sign ($). However, unlike the shell that used the dollar sign for variables, awk doesn't. Variables are simply referenced by their names. For example, to add all numbers in field 5, you can use the variable *mysum* as in this example, *mysum* += $5. Notice that to reference field 5, the dollar sign is needed, but the variable *mysum* is simply the word "mysum," with no special syntax.

The preceding is a basic discussion of awk. Some areas not covered are special input processing, predefined variables, some built-in functions, and array processing.

Note

awk supports the concept of associative arrays. Typically an *array* is a process of storing multiple values; each value is indexed by a number. An *associative array* allows you to store values based on the value of a string or a number; the string becomes the index.

Examples

Suppose you have a church group that periodically likes to visit. People are randomly picked to go to a house called the host. Some of the older members can't handle children in their houses, or maybe their houses are just too small, and some don't feel comfortable having anyone come to their houses, but enjoy visiting others. To control this you maintain a database with people from the church with the following fields.

```
:Bontrager, Bob & Harriet:2:0:y:12:y:10
 ¦      ¦                  ¦ ¦ ¦  ¦  ¦  ¦
 ¦      ¦                  ¦ ¦ ¦  ¦  ¦  ¦->last w/ group
 ¦      ¦                  ¦ ¦ ¦  ¦  ¦ ->can take kids
 ¦      ¦                  ¦ ¦ ¦  ¦->max take
 ¦      ¦                  ¦ ¦ ¦-> will host
 ¦      ¦                  ¦ ¦->number of children in
 ¦      ¦                  ¦      family
 ¦      ¦                  ¦->number of adults in family
 ¦      ¦->name of family
 ¦->indicator that will be host this time, normally blank
```

To get an orderly printout of this, write the following awk script.

```
awk -F: '
BEGIN {
printf("Name                       Adults Kids
➥Will-be-host Max-take Kids-Ok
➥last_with\n\n");
}
```

```
{
if ($5 == "y")                                  #
➡test if they will be a host or not
   {
   HOST="yes";                                  # set
   ➡output value of HOST variable to "yes"
   hosting++                                     #
   ➡increment the hosting variable count by 1
   max_take_tot+=$6                    # add to
   ➡the total number all hosts can take
   }
else
   HOST="no";                                   # if
   ➡not a host then set HOST variable to "no"
if ($7 == "y")                                   #
➡test if they can take kids, and set KIDS
➡appropriately
   KIDS="yes";
else
   KIDS="no";
printf("%-30s%5d%5d       %-5s       %5d   %-5s
➡%5s\n", $2,$3,$4,HOST,$6,KIDS,$8);
                                 # print the formated
                                 ➡output
n_adults+=$3;                                    #
➡add up the total number of adults
n_kids+=$4;                                      #
➡add up the total number of kids
}
END {
printf("\nTotal
➡%5d%5d%22d\n", n_adults, n_kids, (max_take_tot /
➡hosting));
                             # print the totals and the
                             ➡average number of people
                             ➡needed at each host
}
' <data
```

Running the following awk script on the sample data set:

```
:Bontrager, Bob & Harriet:2:0:y:12:y:10
:Bontrager, Fritz & Chris:2:1:y:12:y:11
:Bontreger, Gene & Alma:2:0:y:12:y:1
:Bontreger, Randy & Janis:2:2:y:12:y:6
:Bontreger, Omar & Mary Alice:2:0:y:12:y:2
:Byers, Daryl & Janet:2:2:y:15:y:7
:Chupp, Harvey & Carolyn:2:0:y:12:y:8
:Freed, Lowell:2:5:y:14:y:10
:Fry, Ezra:2:0:y:10:y:1
```

```
:Fry, Olen & Lucy:2:0:n:0:n:5
:Gerber, Walter & Anna:2:0:y:10:y:2
:Guth, Ron & Caryl:1:0:y:25:y:6
:Hochstedler, Cal & Linda:2:3:y:15:y:2
:Hochstedler, Lamar:2:0:y:15:y:2
:Hochstetler, Gene & Beth:2:0:y:10:y:1
:Hochstetler, Lonnie & Shirley:2:0:y:12:y:6
:Hostetler, Bud:2:0:y:10:y:3
:Hostetler, Doug & Dee:2:1:n:0:n:1
:Hostetler, Jim:2:2:y:10:y:3
:Hostetler, Merv & Margaret:2:0:y:12:y:4
:Hostetler, Richard:2:0:y:10:y:6
```

Will produce:

```
Name                          Adults Kids Will-be-
➡host Max-take Kids-Ok last_with

Bontrager, Bob & Harriet         2     0     yes
➡12   yes       10
Bontrager, Fritz & Chris         2     1     yes
➡12   yes       11
Bontreger, Gene & Alma           2     0     yes
➡12   yes       1
Bontreger, Randy & Janis         2     2     yes
➡12   yes       6
Bontreger, Omar & Mary Alice     2     0     yes
➡12   yes       2
Byers, Daryl & Janet             2     2     yes
➡15   yes       7
Chupp, Harvey & Carolyn          2     0     yes
➡12   yes       8
Freed, Lowell                    2     5     yes
➡14   yes       10
Fry, Ezra                        2     0     yes
➡10   yes       1
Fry, Olen & Lucy                 2     0     no
➡0    no        5
Gerber, Walter & Anna            2     0     yes
➡10   yes       2
Guth, Ron & Caryl                1     0     yes
➡25   yes       6
Hochstedler, Cal & Linda         2     3     yes
➡15   yes       2
Hochstedler, Lamar               2     0     yes
➡15   yes       2
Hochstetler, Gene & Beth         2     0     yes
➡10   yes       1
```

```
Hochstetler, Lonnie & Shirley    2    0       yes
➡12   yes      6
Hostetler, Bud                   2    0       yes
➡10   yes      3
Hostetler, Doug & Dee            2    1       no
➡0    no       1
Hostetler, Jim                   2    2       yes
➡10   yes      3
Hostetler, Merv & Margaret       2    0       yes
➡12   yes      4
Hostetler, Richard               2    0       yes
➡10   yes      6

Total                           41   16
12
```

The preceding example doesn't use pattern matching. You can modify it as follows to print out any of the Frys.

```
awk -F: '
BEGIN {
printf("Name                          Adults Kids
➡Will-be-host Max-take Kids-Ok last_with\n\n");
}
 /Fry/ {
 ➡#only look for the names with Fry
if ($5 == "y")                                      #
➡test if they will be a host or not
   {
   HOST="yes";                              # set
   ➡output value of HOST variable to "yes"
   hosting++                                #
   ➡increment the hosting variable count by 1
   max_take_tot+=$6               # add to
   ➡the total number all hosts can take
   }
else
   HOST="no";                               # if
   ➡not a host then set HOST variable to "no"
if ($7 == "y")                                      #
➡test if they can take kids, and set KIDS
➡appropriately
   KIDS="yes";
else
   KIDS="no";
printf("%-30s%5d%5d        %-5s      %5d    %-5s
➡%5s\n", $2,$3,$4,HOST,$6,KIDS,$8);
                             # print the formated
                             ➡output
```

```
n_adults+=$3;                                    #
➥add up the total number of adults
n_kids+=$4;                                      #
add up the total number of kids
}
END {
printf("\nTotal
➥%5d%5d%22d\n", n_adults, n_kids, (max_take_tot /
hosting));
                              # print the totals and the
                              ➥average number of people
                              ➥needed at each host
}
' <data
```

Results in:

```
Name                        Adults Kids Will-be-
➥host Max-take Kids-Ok last_with


Fry, Ezra                     2    0       yes
10   yes        1
Fry, Olen & Lucy              2    0       no
0    no         5

Total                         4    0
10
```

See also

ed, sed, sh, ksh, csh, cut, paste, grep

banner

banner produces an "enlarged" version of the arguments
passed to it. As many as 10 characters may be specified.
These characters are then enlarged using a series of aster-
isks(*). The output of banner is the standard output.

Syntax

banner *strings*

Argument or Option	Description
strings	The list of 10 character strings to create a banner. Each string, if separated by a space, creates a banner on successive lines. Two strings may be enclosed in quotation marks ("), which causes banner to place the strings on the same line.

Note

The lp spooler uses banner to print the banner page, typically passing banner the login id of the user requesting the print-out.

Examples

```
banner hello
```

Produces the word hello in a larger format to the standard output.

```
banner "My Banner" ¦ lp
```

Prints My Banner on the default printer.

basename

Extracts the filename portion of path name. You can also strip off trailing characters or extensions.

Syntax

```
basename pathname extension
```

Argument or Option	Description
pathname	The path name of the file of which you want the basename.
extension	The extension or suffix to strip off.

Examples

```
basename /usr/acct/frank
```

The result displayed on the standard output is frank.

```
basename /usr/acct/frank/bowling.wk3 .wk3
```

The result displayed on the standard output is bowling. Notice how the characters .wk3 are stripped from the output.

Tip

Suppose you copy Frank's home directory to Pete's and then discover that you shouldn't have. Because you can't delete all Pete's home directory, you have to delete each file one at a time. When used with the shell's output assignment operator ('), basename is a powerful tool when writing shell scripts. The following deletes all files found in Frank's home directory from Pete's home directory.

```
for i in /usr/acct/frank/*
do
rm /usr/acct/pete/'basename $i'
done
```

See also

dirname

batch

See at.

bc

bc is a calculator program offering not only the ease of
simple math operations, but also a programming language
similar to C in construct. bc is particularly useful for base
conversions. For a complete list of operators and structures
consult the User's Reference supplied with your system or
the on-line man pages.

Syntax:

```
bc -c -l filelist
```

Argument or Option	Description
-c	Normally, bc acts as a preprocessor for the dc (desk calculator). This option sends the "compiled" output to the standard output instead of dc.
-l	Enables access to the math library that includes the trigonometric and logarithmic functions.
filelist	The list of files containing bc functions to be executed. After executing the list of files, bc reads from the standard input. This enables you to load the functions with which you have to work from a set of files and then to interactively call on these functions.

Examples

The following example multiplies 40 times 512. The result (20480) is displayed on the next line.

```
bc
40*512
20480
^D
```

The next several examples are base conversions from one number system to another. In each of these, the word ibase refers to the input base, and the word obase refers to the output base.

Text converts the base 16 (hex) number 1B to its decimal equivalent.

```
bc
ibase=16
1B
27
^D
```

The following example converts from base 16 to base 2 (binary).

```
bc
ibase=16
obase=2
1B
11011
^D
```

This example sets the scaling to 4 decimals and calculates the result of 2 divided by 3.

```
bc
scale=4
2/3
.6666
^D
```

Message

```
cannot open input file on line 1, badfilename
```

You supplied bc with a file name that it cannot open.

See also

dc

bdiff

Runs diff on files that are too large for it. bdiff breaks up the two files for comparison into smaller chunks. The output is merged and the line numbers adjusted as if diff had been run directly.

Syntax

```
bdiff file1 file2 lines -s
```

Argument or Option	Description
file1	The first file used in the comparison. If a dash (–) is used then standard input is read.
file2	The second file used in the comparison. If a dash (–) is used then standard input is read.
lines	The number of lines to send to diff at a time. The default is 3500.
-s	Suppresses the printing of bdiff diagnostics. This does not stop the printing of diff diagnostics, however.

Rule

Because the file is broken up into pieces, bdiff may not be able to find a minimum number of differences.

Messages

```
ERROR: arg counter(bd1)
```

You didn't supply bdiff with the right number of arguments.

```
ERROR: 'filename' non-existent( (ut4)
```

The file name you supplied bdiff doesn't exist.

Example

```
bdiff letter-to-mom letter-to-mom.old
```

Passes the two files to diff for comparison after breaking them up into 3500 line pieces. (These were presumably very long letters.)

See also

diff, split

cal

cal displays a calendar on the standard output. The output is small. One year takes less than one 8 1/2-by-11-inch sheet of paper. This can be useful when you have to quickly compare several years or want to find out on what day of the week a particular date occurs.

Syntax

```
cal month year
```

Argument or Option	Description
month	May be a number between 1 and 12, or enough letters to represent a unique month. (J is not enough to distinguish January, June, and July.) The default is the current month.
year	May be any number between 1 and 9999. The default is the current year. All four numbers of the year must be specified. That is, 92 refers to the year 92 not 1992.

Note

When no arguments are given, the current month plus the previous and the next are displayed along with the current date and time.

Messages

```
cal: bad year 0
```

This message tells you the year 0 cannot be printed. The year must be between 1 and 9999.

```
cal: non-unique month name Ma
```

Here you only supplied the letters Ma, and cal can't determine if you wanted May or March.

Examples

```
cal
```

Shows the current month plus the previous month and the next month.

```
cal 1960
```

Shows the calendar for the year 1960.

```
cal 10 1994
```

Shows the month of October for 1994.

calendar

Produces a to-do list by reading the file calendar in your current directory.

Syntax

```
calendar -
```

Argument or Option	Description
- (hyphen)	When this argument is given calendar looks in every user's home directory for the file calendar and mails them the results.

Rules

To be mailed a "to-do" list you have to have a file called calendar created in your home directory. In this file you can list one-line entries containing the date that the task or appointment is on. You may specify multiple lines for the same task. Each line, however, must contain the date or that line is not mailed.

calendar accepts the following date formats:

```
12/25/91
Dec 25 1991
Dec 25
```

However, 25 Dec is not acceptable.

`calendar` mails you the lines found in the `calendar` file one day before the date and on the date. Friday is considered to be one date before Monday. No similar adjustment is made for holidays.

The `calendar` file must have public read permissions for the `calendar` utility to be able to access the information.

Tip

You can make this process automatic by adding the following line to your `crontab` for root.

```
0 1 * * * calendar -
```

This way each day at 1:00 a.m. `calendar` runs—searching each user's home directory and mailing them their appointments.

Example

```
calendar
```

Gives you a list of the tasks and appointments in your `calendar` file.

See also

cron, mail

cancel

Cancels a print request generated by the `lp` spooler.

Syntax

```
cancel request-ids
```

```
cancel printer
```

Argument or Option	Description
request-ids	This is a list of 1p spooler request ids. The 1p spooler assigns a unique id to each print request. To list the request id use lpstat.
printer	The name of the printer to which print requests go. If a printer name is specified, then the job currently printing is canceled.

Notes

Unless you are the super user or an 1p administrator, you may only cancel the jobs you have requested.

If the job is currently printing, a message regarding its termination is printed on the paper. Also, if a print request is canceled by someone other than yourself, you are informed by system mail as to who canceled the job and what request id was canceled.

Messages

```
cancel: "bad-id" is not a request id or a printer
```

You have tried to cancel a print request that doesn't exist or have given cancel a bad printer name.

```
cancel: request "bad-id" is non-existent
```

You have given cancel an id that doesn't exist.

Examples

```
cancel frontdsk-107
```

Cancels the print request that is going to the frontdsk printer.

```
cancel frontdsk
```

Cancels the currently printing job on the `frontdsk` printer.

Tips

If the job you want to cancel is currently printing, the termination message is printed and the next job begins to print immediately. The paper does not advance to the top of form. A good practice to adopt is to first disable the printer; this stops the printing of the current request and stops the printing of all jobs on that printer until it is enabled again. You can then cancel the request, realign the printer to top of form, and then enable the printer.

See also

lp, lpstat, disable, enable

cat

Concatenates files. This is sometimes used to display a file.

Syntax

```
cat [flags] filelist
```

Argument or Option	Description
filelist	This is an optional list of files to concatenate. If no files are specified or a dash (-) is specified, the standard input is read.

Flags

Argument or Option	Description
-s	Suppresses messages about unreadable files.
-u	Causes the output to be unbuffered.
-v	Displays the control characters with a caret(^) before the character that was used to generate the character (for example, an end-of-text, 04, displays as ^D). Characters above octal 0177—the Del character—are displayed with an M- in front of the character that has a high bit set to generate the character. Tabs and formfeeds are not affected by this option.
-t	Valid only with the -v option, this causes the tabs and formfeeds to be displayed in the -v format as well.
-e	Valid only with the -v option, newlines are preceded by the dollar sign ($).

    -n   number each line of output

Note

An output file name must not be the same as any of the input names unless it is a special file.

Messages

```
cat: illegal option -- -badoption
```

You invoked cat with an option other than those listed previously. -badoption is replaced with the option you specified.

```
cat: cannot open badfile
```

You invoked cat with a file name that can't be opened.

```
cat: input filename is output
```

You specified an output file name that was used in the input (for example, `cat myfile hisfile >myfile`).

Examples

    cat letter-to-dad

Concatenates `letter-to-dad` with nothing and sends the output to the screen.

    cat letter-to-dad signature >send.let

Appends the file `signature` to `letter-to-dad` and creates a new file called `send.let`.

Tip

`cat` is a powerful, yet simple utility that I have used to capture the printout from an old machine for which no other suitable media exchange existed. I merely plugged the serial cable into the appropriate port and typed something similar to this: `cat </dev/tty1a >my-file`. This allowed my UNIX machine to be the "printer" for the old machine and logged the output to the file `myfile`.

See also

    echo, pr, pg, more, cp

cd

Changes the current working directory.

Syntax

    cd dirname

Argument or Option	Description
dirname	Changes to an optional directory name. If no directory is specified, the user is returned to his home directory.

Note

You must have execute permissions on the directory to which you wish to change.

Messages

baddir: bad directory

You have specified a directory that doesn't exist.

cd */dir*?

If you type a directory to change to and misspell the directory name, cd prompts you with what it thought you might have meant. */dir* is replaced with the directory cd thinks you mean. Any response not starting with an *n* is assumed to be yes, thus simply pressing return accepts the prompt.

See also

pwd, sh, chmod, ls

checkmail

checkmail reports the status of mail you sent that hasn't reached its destination.

Syntax

checkmail -a -f

When invoked with no arguments, `checkmail` shows the subject of messages and shows the addresses that did not receive them.

Argument or Option	Description
-a	Causes both delivered and undelivered addresses to appear on the report. Depending on the system configuration, the delivered addresses may not be accessible due to the mail system cleaning up after itself.
-f	The "fast" mode that suppresses the printing of the subject line. Only the addresses appear on the report.

Tip

If mail remains in the queue, it is usually because a host is down.

See also

mail

chgrp

Changes the group ownership of a file.

Syntax

```
chgrp group filelist
```

Argument or Option	Description
group	The group to change to. This may either be the numerical value of the group id, or the name as found in the file /etc/group.
filelist	A space separated list of files of which to change the group ownership.

Note

You may not change the group ownership of a file unless you are the owner of the file or the super user.

Messages

    chgrp: unknown group: *badgroupid*

You entered a group id that doesn't exit, *badgroupid* is substituted with the bad group id you supplied.

    badfile: no such file or directory

You supplied chgrp with a file name that doesn't exist.

Example

    chgrp sales /usr/salesstuff/*

Changes all the files found in the salesstuff directory to the group ownership of sales.

See also

    chown, chmod

chmod

Changes the mode of files. The mode of a file controls the
access permissions associated with that file. UNIX has three
levels of security: ownership, group access, and everyone
else. Within these three levels are three permissions: read,
write, and execute. On standard files the read permission
means you are able to look at the contents of that file, the
write permission enables you to modify the file, and the
execute permission means you can execute it. Directories
behave only slightly differently. The read permission enables
you to view the contents of the directory—an ls command
works. The write permission enables you to create new files
in the directory and to delete files from the directory. Finally
the execute permission means you can change directory to
the directory—the cd command works.

Syntax

    chmod *mode filelist*

    chmod *level action permission filelist*

There are two formats. The first is less complicated but requires knowledge of the valid numbers to set the various
permissions. It is the "absolute" method. It sets the permissions at all levels. The second format is more complicated
but lets you use symbols to specify the permissions, and they
are specified incrementally. This is the "relative" method
because you can add or remove permissions.

Argument or Option	Description
filelist	Lists the files affected by the chmod command.

Argument or Option	Description
mode	The numeric mode, in octal, of the permissions this file has for all levels. Each octal number sets a bit in the mode field stored in the i-node table of the file system. Adding the numbers together sets the combination of the permissions. The permissions at the user/owner, group, and other/world levels all follow the same pattern. An additional level controls some special handling. The mode is in the following form: SUGO, where S=special, U=user/owner, G=group, and O=others/world. Each number may be any from the following table (consult the user's reference provided with your system for the Special meaning of the numbers as they differ from the U, G, and O meanings).

Value	Permission
0	None!
1	Execute
2	~~Read~~ write
4	~~Write~~ Read

(handwritten margin notes: "1 Huge mistake Read=4 write=2")

level	The level affected by the rest of the command. It can be any character listed in the following table:

Code	Meaning
u	The user/owner of the file
g	The group level
o	Others or the world level
a	All of levels. Default if nothing for *level* is specified.

(continues)

Argument or Option	Description
action	Specifies what action takes place on the mode of the file. It can be any character listed in the following table:

Code	Meaning
+	Adds the permission
-	Removes the permission
=	Sets the permission to only what is specified.

Argument or Option	Description
permission	The permission to apply to the file. It can be one or more listed in the ` following table:

Code	Permission granted
r	read
w	write
x	execute

Message

```
chmod: ERROR: invalid mode
```

You didn't specify the mode correctly. Check each portion of the command again. The second form of the command must use the rules described previously. You may have typed the wrong thing.

Examples

```
chmod 777 letter-to-dad
```

Enables letter-to-dad to have all permissions at all levels. Notice how the "special" level isn't specified; this is an implied 0 and no special permissions are granted. The execute permission, in this case, is nonsense; however, it demonstrates the use of the 7 to mean all possible permissions.

```
chmod 644 letter-to-dad
```

Allows every one to read `letter-to-dad` but only the owner can change it.

```
chmod a+w letter-to-dad
```

Adds the write permission to the letter for everyone.

```
chmod o-wr,g-wr letter-to-dad
```

Removes both read and write permissions at both the group and other levels.

```
chmod o=r letter-to-dad
```

Sets the other level to allow reading only. All other permissions at this level are taken away.

See also

umask, ls

chown

Enables you to change the ownership of the file. In a sense, you are giving the file to someone else.

Syntax

```
chown user filelist
```

Argument or Option	Description
user	May be a numerical user id or a valid user name as found in the /etc/passwd file.
filelist	The space separated list of files of which to reassign the ownership.

Note

The ownership of the file can only be changed by the owner or the super user. However, if you are the owner of a file and you assign that file to another user, you can't change your mind and reassign it to yourself because you are no longer the owner.

Messages

```
badfile: No such file or directory
```

You specified a file in *filelist* that doesn't exist, *badfile* is substituted with the file you specified.

```
chown: unknown userid baduserid
```

You used a user name not found in /etc/passwd. *baduserid* is substituted with the user name you specified.

Example

```
chown pete/usr/acct/pete/*
```

This example changes all the files found in pete's home directory to the ownership of pete.

See also

chgrp

clear

Clears the screen, or if you are working at a hard copy terminal, this command formfeeds the paper.

Syntax

```
clear term
```

Argument or Option	Description
term	If not specified, the environment variable TERM is used. Must match a valid entry in the file /etc/termcap.

Note

The c1 termcap type can be defined in the /etc/termcap file. If not, then a series of newlines are sent.

Example

```
clear
```

Clears the screen and leaves the prompt in the upper left corner.

See also

```
echo
```

cmp

Compares two files.

Syntax

```
cmp -l -s file1 file2
```

Argument or Option	Description
file1	A valid file name or the dash (-) to have cmp read from the standard input.

(continues)

Argument or Option	Description
file2	A valid file name.
-1	Causes cmp to list the offset (in decimal form) of the files where a difference occurs, and to list the differing bytes (in octal form).
-s	Tells cmp not to produce output. cmp sets only an exit status (0=no differences, 1=the files are different, and 2=inaccessible or missing file).

Messages

```
cmp: EOF on file
```

One file is shorter than the other. *file* becomes the name of the shorter file.

```
cmp: cannot open file
```

Access to the file is not possible, the file may not exist, or you don't have read permissions. *file* becomes the file you specified to open.

Example

```
cmp letter-to-mom letter.save
```

Compares the letter (letter-to-mom) with a letter named (letter.save).

Tip

The cmp command is best suited for binary files; diff is better suited for text files. If you want to know only if two files are identical, and don't care why they are different, cmp works fine.

See also

diff, diff3, sdiff, comm

comm

comm finds common lines in two sorted files. The command generates three columns of information: the lines found only in the first file, those found only in the second file, and the lines found in both files.

Syntax

```
comm [flags] file1 file2
```

Argument or Option	Description
file1	The first file to use in the comparison. You can specify the dash (-) if you want comm to read the standard input.
file2	The second file to use in the comparison.

Flags

Argument or Option	Description
-1	Doesn't produce the first column.
-2	Doesn't produce the second column.
-3	Doesn't produce the third column.

Message

```
comm: cannot open badfilename
```

You gave `comm` a file name that doesn't exist or that you don't have permission to read. `badfilename` becomes the file name you specified to open.

Examples

```
ls /usr/sue >sue.dir
ls /usr/frank >frank.dir
comm sue.dir frank.dir
```

Stores the directory listings of files found in two users' accounts. If `frank` and `sue` work on files with similar names, you can find out what the files have in common. (`dircmp` is actually a better tool for this task—for example, `dircmp/usr /sue/usr/frank`).

```
comm -12 sue.dir frank.dir
```

Uses the same directory listings as in the previous command. In this example, output is limited to those files that have something in common.

See also

diff, sdiff, sort, uniq, cmp, dircmp

compress

`compress` allows you to compress or reduce the amount of disk space a file uses. Sometimes you have files in your directories that you don't need to access often, but that you don't want to remove. You can use `compress` to make these files smaller, and make room for other files. Compressing files also reduces the amount of time it takes to send them across a modem.

Syntax

```
compress [-cdfFqv ] file-list

uncompress [ -fqc ] file-list

zcat file-list
```

Argument or Option	Description
file-list	A space separated list of files to compress/uncompress.

Flags

Argument or Option	Description
c	Writes the result of compress/ uncompress to standard output without altering the original file. Allows compress and uncompress to be used as a filter in a pipeline.
d	Decompresses the file and expands it to its original size. It makes compress behave like uncompress.
f	Forces the output file to be overwritten even if it already exists. Normally compress creates a file with a .Z suffix. Without this flag set, if a file already exists with a .Z suffix, you are prompted to overwrite the files. This flag forces the file to be overwritten without a need for your response.
F	Forces the output file to be written even if no file savings take place. Normally, compress does not create a file with the .Z suffix unless compression actually saves space. This flag forces creation of a .Z suffix file even though no savings take place.

(continues)

Argument or Option	Description
q	Quiet mode. The opposite of -v, nothing displays except error messages.
v	Verbose mode. Displays the name of the file being compressed and the percentage of compression. When used with uncompress, only the file name displays.

Rules

compress cannot compress files with links; if you attempt to do so you get an error message. If you compress a file with a symbolic link, the link is broken, and you end up with a compressed copy of the file; the pointer no longer exists to the original file.

If no file is specified on the command line, then the standard input is used. This, along with the -c flag, allows compress to be easily integrated into a pipeline of commands.

Normally compress creates a file with the suffix of .Z when the -c option is not specified. These files retain the owner-ship and permissions of the original file. When you use the -c flag, the file created has your default permissions and you are the owner of the file.

When passing *file-list* to uncompress and zcat, the .Z suffix is assumed. For example, if you compress the file letter_dad, you end up with a file called: letter_dad.Z. When you want to uncompress this file, you need only type: uncompress letter_dad. uncompress looks for a file with the .Z suffix.

Messages

    hello: No such file or directory

You attempted to compress a file named hello that doesn't exist.

```
ben: Compression: -2.22% -- file unchanged
data: Compression: 41.20% -- replaced with data.Z
print: Compression: 29.09% -- replaced with print.Z
tst: Compression: -14.63% -- file unchanged
```

An example of using the -v flag. Note how the files ben and tst do not result in a file savings; the original file remains intact. The -F flag wasn't used.

```
ben.Z: No such file or directory
```

You attempted to uncompress a file called ben.z but it does not exist.

```
data:   -- has 1 other links: unchanged
```

You attempted to compress a file called data and this file had a link to some other file.

```
data.Z: already has .Z suffix -- no change
```

You attempted to compress a file (data.z) which already had the .z suffix.

Examples

```
compress *
```

Compresses everything in the current directory.

```
uncompress *.Z
```

Uncompresses everything with a .z suffix.

```
zcat *.Z
```

Uncompresses and displays the contents of all files with a .z suffix and leaves the original file intact.

See also

pack, pcat, unpack, cat

copy

Copies files or entire directory structures, keeping the same ownership, permissions, and modification times.

Syntax

```
copy [flags] sources destination
```

Argument or Option	Description
sources	A space separated list of files or directories to be copied.
destination	The directory or file to which to copy.

Flags

Argument or Option	Description
-a	Asks for confirmation before each copy. Any response beginning with a *y* is assumed to be a yes; any other response is assumed to be a no.
-l	Uses links instead of copies whenever possible. This is not possible with directories. (This option, if links are possible, is significantly faster because copies of the data are not made.) See Chapter 6 for more information on links.
-n	Copies the file only if it is new. If the destination file already exists, then the copy isn't performed.

Argument or Option	Description
-o	Keeps the original owner and group ownerships of the copied files. Otherwise, the file's owner and group become the user who is running the copy procedure.
-m	When the files are copied, they keep their modification times; otherwise, they are set to the time of the copy.
-r	This recursively traverses directories, copying each file and directory encountered.
-v	Displays the files copied by copy.

Message

```
copy: cannot open badfilename
```

You tried to copy a file that doesn't exist or you don't have permission to read; *badfilename* is substituted with the name you supplied.

Examples

```
copy * /tmp/temp
```

Copies all the files in the current directory to the /tmp/temp directory. It also copies the first files found in any sub-directories into the current directory. (For example, suppose the current directory has a subdirectory called play and in the play subdirectory, there is a file called rules and a directory called games. The file rules is copied, but the contents of games are not; you must use the -r flag to copy the subdirectory's contents.)

```
copy -r . /tmp/temp
```

Recursively copies the current directory to the directory
/tmp/temp. A duplicate of the directory structures is made.

Caution

The documentation provided in the user's reference provided
with the system states that entire file system may be copied.
In the general sense this is not true. When you have files in a
file system, links may be created within the file system, and
links are not preserved across file systems. If copy were used
to move a file system, then the links are lost. The following
cpio command, however, preserves the links:

```
find . -depth -print ¦ cpio -pamdlv /my-new-filesystem
```

Copies all files found in the current directory to the new file
system.

See also

cp, ln, cpio, mv

cp

Copies files. You may copy one file to another file, or a list of
files to a directory.

Syntax

cp *source-file dest-file*

cp *source-list dest-directory*

Argument or Option	Description
source-file	The file to copy.
dest-file	The destination name. This may be a directory name, as well, in which case the source file name is used as the name and the file is placed in this directory.
source-list	A space separated list of files to copy.
dest-directory	The destination directory.

Examples

```
cp letter-to-dad letter.save
```

Copies `letter-to-dad` to a file called `letter.save`.

```
cp letter* /old-letters
```

Copies all the files starting with the word `letter` to a directory called `old-letters`.

Caution

No verification is done of a file of the same name already existing in the destination. Therefore, if you aren't careful, you can end up overwriting a file in the destination you need.

See also

rm, copy, ln, mv

cpio

cpio stands for copy in out. It is useful not only for making backups, but also for moving files around the file system.

Syntax

```
cpio -o [flags]

cpio -i [flags] filelist

cpio -p [flags] dirname
```

Argument or Option	Description
-o	Creates the archive. You are generating the output. cpio accepts its list of files to backup from the standard input.
-i	Copies in from a previously created archive (that is, the -o option).
-p	Accepts a list of files from the standard input and passes them to the specified directory. Useful for copying entire directory structures on the file system.
filelist	A space separated list of files to extract from the archive. May contain wild cards. The wild cards supported are the same as the simple regular expression expansion provided by the shell (sh).

	!	means not
	?	matches a single character
	*	matches any number of characters
	[]	matches the set of characters specified between the brackets

Argument or Option	Description
	If you use wild cards, enclose *filelist* in quotation marks ("); otherwise, the shell expands these wild cards and not cpio. A weakness of another archiver, tar, is that it doesn't support wild cards; it has to rely on the shell for wild-card expansion to generate a list of files.
dirname	The destination directory for the files given cpio with the -p option.

Flags

Argument or Option	Description
-B	Signifies a blocking factor of 5,120 bytes per record. Used with the -o and -i options and only when sending the output to, or reading the input from, a character special device (for example, tape, or floppy).
-C*buff-size*	Functionally equivalent to -B, but allows you to specify the buffer size to use. *buff-size* is normally the number of bytes. When used with the -K option, *buff-size* is interpreted as a multiple of 1,024 bytes or 1K.
-a	Reset the access times of the files after the copy is completed. If used with -l, the files with links are not affected. Used with -o or -i.

(continues)

Argument or Option	Description
-c	Creates and reads the header information in the archive in an ASCII character format. This creates headers readable on other platforms. For example, you can move an archive created on an X86 Intel-based machine to a 68X Motorola-based machine. Used with -o or -i.
-d	Creates the directories as needed. If the directories don't exist, cpio creates them. Used with -p or -i.
-b	Reverses the order of bytes within a word. -b is used with the -i option only.
-f	Enables you to change the interpretation of *filelist*. Normally *filelist* is a list of files to extract. When the -f option is used, *filelist* is the list of files not to extract. Used with -i.
-K *volsize*	Specifies the size of the source or destination volume. *volsize* is a number representing the size in kilobytes. Useful when reading or writing to removable media (for example, tapes or floppy disks) as you are prompted to insert the next one.
-l	Links files rather than copying them, if possible. Used with -p.
-m	Retains the modification times of the files as found in the archive. Normally the modification times change to the current time. This has no effect on directories. Used with -i and -p.
-r	Renames the files in filelist. You are prompted for each file in filelist for the new name. If none is given, the file is skipped. Used with -o or -i.

Argument or Option	Description
-t	Prints a list of the files in the archive. Used with -i.
-u	Extracts the files from the archive unconditionally. Normally cpio only extracts the file from the archive if the file in the archive has a newer modification time than the one on the file system. Used with -p or -i.
-v	Signifies verbose mode. Tells cpio to give status reporting on what it is doing. Used with -i.

Message

The message you are most likely to see is a usage clause showing you the necessary syntax to use cpio. If you get this message you probably forgot to provide an option that was needed. Check your command line again.

Examples

```
ls ¦ cpio -oBc >/dev/rdsk/5h
```

Lists the current directory, passing the list through the pipeline to cpio. cpio uses the input from the pipeline as its list of files to copy. It copies this list of files to the standard output with a blocking factor of 5120 and the header information is written in a portable ASCII format. This output is then redirected to the character special device /dev/rdsk/5h (a high-density 5 1/4-inch floppy disk).

```
cpio -iBcdm "*.ltr" </dev/rdsk/5h
```

Extracts only the files ending in .ltr from the floppy disk, placing them in the current directory. Any subdirectories are created as needed. The file's modification times are the same as they were at the time the archive was created.

```
ls -A ¦ cpio -pdl /usr/newdir
```

This command takes the list generated by `ls` and copies it to the directory `/usr/newdir`, creating any directories needed and linking instead of copying when possible.

Tip

`cpio` with the `-i` and `-o` options is a filter program, meaning that it accepts its input from the standard input and directs its output to the standard output. This means that `cpio` can be anywhere in the pipeline, as long as the input to the `-o` option is a list of file names, and the input to the `-i` option is the result of a previous `-o`. The `-p` option is not a true filter, because the output is the specified directory.

See also

copy, tar, find

cron

A background program started by the system to manage scheduled execution of programs. The system comes installed with `cron`; it runs continuously. You should never have to type this command. `cron` allows you to schedule when jobs will take place by reading a file in `/usr/spool` `/cron/crontabs/`*username*, where *username* becomes the name of a user who is allowed to run a job.

Syntax

```
cron
```

Rule

To use cron you must have your user name in the file /usr
/lib/cron/cron.allow. Some sites may have the file /usr/lib
/cron/cron.deny. At these sites, users on this list cannot use
cron.

See also

crontab, at, batch

crontab

Informs cron of the programs and the schedule on which
they should be run.

Syntax

crontab *sched-file*

crontab -l

crontab -r

Argument or Option	Description
sched-file	The name of a file containing the schedule and programs to run. If no file is given, crontab reads from the standard input. The file must be in the following format: M H D m d *cmd*.
	M The minute of the hour (0-59).
	H The hour of the day (0-23).
	D The day of the month (1-31).
	m The month of the year (1-12).

(continues)

Argument or Option	Description
	d The day of the week. (0-6, 0=Sunday)
	cmd The program to run; the string passed to sh.
	The first five fields may be a single digit, a list of digits separated by commas, a range of digits using a dash, or an asterisk (meaning all legal values).
-l	Lists what you have told cron to do.
-r	Removes your jobs from cron's tables; cron no longer executes those jobs.

Rule

All jobs are executed with sh from your home directory ($HOME). The environment is setup with HOME, LOGNAME, SHELL= /BIN/SH, and PATH=/bin:usr/bin. If you need your .profile run to set additional environment variables, you have to do this specifically in the crontab *sched-file*.

Messages

    crontab: you are not authorized to use cron. Sorry.

You are not allowed to use cron. Check the cron.deny and cron.allow files.

    crontab: can't open your crontab file

You don't currently have a crontab file defined and either tried to list it using the -l flag, or you simply gave a bad flag and crontab thought this was a file name.

```
* * * * echo hello
crontab: error on previous line: unexpected
➥character found in line.
```

You receive this message when your *sched-file* is not properly defined. In the example, the file has a line in it without sufficient fields. When this happens, cron ignores the entire file. You must change and resubmit the file.

Examples

```
0 8 * * * echo "Good Morning"
0 8 25 12 * echo "Merry Christmas"
0 8 * * 1 echo "Not Monday again"
```

Here are some examples of what the *sched-file* might contain. The first line gives the message of "Good Morning" every day at 8:00 a.m. The second line sends "Merry Christmas" once a year on the 25th of December at 8:00 a.m. (Hopefully, you won't be at work to get it.) And the last line complains about it being Monday once a week on Monday morning at 8:00 a.m.

```
crontab exmpl-crontab
```

Reads in a file called exmpl-crontab in the current directory and informs cron that the jobs found in it are to be executed.

```
crontab -l
```

Lists the jobs you asked cron to execute.

```
crontab -r
```

Informs cron to remove your jobs from its scheduling list. You must resubmit a *sched-file* for cron to execute your jobs again.

See also

cron, sh, at

crypt

Encrypts a file. crypt uses a password to store a file in an encrypted form and requires the same password to decode the file. crypt reads from standard input and writes to standard output.

Syntax

    crypt *password*

Argument or Option	Description
password	The password used to gain access to the file. It is also referred to as the encryption key. If you do not supply *password*, crypt prompts you for it.

Rules

crypt generates files compatible with the editors: ed, edit, ex, and vi when in encryption mode.

crypt, although documented, is not distributed with UNIX. This is because the U.S. Government regulates the distribution of the crypt libraries and crypt is not available outside the United States and its territories. Contact your dealer to obtain these tools.

Examples

    crypt pickles <letter-to-mom >let.crypt

Encrypts the letter using the password of pickles and stores the result in the file let.crypt

    crypt pickles <let.crypt ¦ lp

Decodes the previously encrypted file and prints it.

See also

ed, edit, vi, ex

csh

csh is a command interpreter similar to sh. It is named the C-shell because its syntax resembles that of the C programming language. Like sh, csh is almost a complete programming language itself. To take complete advantage of csh, consult the reference manual and user's guide supplied with your system, or consult a book that covers csh exclusively.

Syntax

csh

Examples

csh

Launches a new shell to work in temporarily. When you exit this shell, your environment is returned to what it was before you launched the new shell.

See also

ksh, sh

cu

Dials into other systems, either through a modem or a direct connect. cu also provides a set of tilde (~) commands to enhance its usefulness.

Syntax

```
cu [flags] system-name

cu [flags] -lline -sspeed telno

cu [flags] -lline -sspeed dir
```

Argument or Option	Description
system-name	The name of the system to call. This requires system-name to be setup in the file /usr/lib/uucp /Systems. The speed, line, and phone number are pulled from this file.
-lline	The device used for the communication link.
-sspeed	The baud rate at which to make the connection. If this option is not used, the speed is pulled from the file /usr/lib/uucp/Devices.
telno	The telephone number to dial for automatic dialer. A = indicates second dial tone, a - indicates four-second delay.
dir	A keyword used to inform cu that you want to talk directly with the modem. This is useful when you have to program the modem.

Flags

Argument or Option	Description
-xdebug-level	Sets cu into a debugging level to give diagnostics on its progress. Normally, cu operates silently, and you don't know what it is doing. debug-level may be any digit between 0 and 9; 9 gives the most information.

Argument or Option	Description
-n	Prompts for a telephone number.
-o	The connection is made with odd parity.
-e	The connection is made with even parity.
-oe	The connection is made with 7 data bits and no parity.

Notes

The system administrator must have properly installed the modems and configured the uucp subsystem to use the modems. At a minimum, the devices connected to the modems have to be setup in the file /usr/lib/uucp/Devices.

cu offers several tilde commands. These commands can be used while running cu. Each command is preceded by a tilde (~).

Each time you connect to succesive machines, you need to chain enough tildes to make that command active on the machine you are on. For example, you call the machine "french" and then from french, you call "german." In order for the tilde commands to apply to the machine "german," you need to have two tildes (~~). The following table lists the tilde commands available.

Item	Description
~.	Disconnects from themachine, or quits cu. This is extremely useful if you have to abort a program running on the remote system, or if for some reason, you can't log on.

(continues)

Item	Description
~!	Runs a subshellon the local system.
~!command	Runs command on the local system.
~%command	Runscommand on the local system and sends the results to the remote system.
~%break	Sends a break signal to the remote system. This is useful when the speed at which you dialed in is not the speed at which the port is currently set. A break on UNIX systems causes a new baud rate to be selected.
~%b	Same as ~%break.

Messages

```
Connect failed: SYSTEM NOT IN Systems FILE
```

You gave cu a system name it doesn't recognize. uuname may be used to obtain a list of valid system names on your system.

```
Connect failed: NO DEVICES AVAILABLE
```

All the modems are in use.

Examples

```
cu sosco
```

Calls the system sosco.

```
cu -x9 sosco
```

Calls the system sosco with a debugging level of 9.

```
cu -l/dev/tty1A -s38400 555-1122
```

This command calls the phone number 555-1122 using the modem attached to the port /dev/tty1A at 38400 baud.

```
cu -1/dev/tty1A -s38400 dir
```

This command makes a connection with the modem to program it or test it out.

See also

uucp, uuname

cut

Extracts fields from a list of files. Fields may be defined as either character positions, or relatively, with a field separator.

Syntax

```
cut -cchar-pos filelist
cut -ffields -dfield-sep -s filelist
```

Argument or Option	Description
filelist	The list of files from which to cut. If no files are specified, cut reads from the standard input.
-cchar-pos	The character position to cut out. May be a list separated by commas (,), or a range separated by dashes (-), or a combination. (For example, 1, 4, 5 or 1-4 or 1-4, 5-10, 25 are all valid).
-ffields	The fields to cut out. Fields are denoted by a one character separator. If the separator repeats, as in several in a row, they are not treated as one separator. fields uses the same syntax as char-pos.

(continues)

Argument or Option	Description
-d*field-sep*	Specifies the field separator. A tab character is the default. *field-sep* may be any character.
-s	Suppress the line if it doesn't contain *field-sep* characters.

Note

The -c and -f options are mutually exclusive.

Messages

```
line too long
```

One of the input lines from one of the files was longer than 511 characters.

```
bad list for c/f options
```

You didn't supply cut with either a -c or -f flag, or the *char-pos/fields* were incorrectly specified.

```
no fields
```

You didn't supply *char-pos* or *fields*.

Example

```
cut -f1,5 -d: /etc/passwd
```

Extracts the user id and names from the password file.

See also

paste

date

Displays the system date and time, or if you are the super user, sets the date and time. You can control how the date is displayed.

Syntax

```
date MMDDhhmmYY

date +format
```

Argument or Option	Description
MMDDhhmmYY	This is the format used to set the date and time. The following table explains each variable. Each part must be two digits.
	MM The month (01–12).
	DD The day (01–31).
	hh The hour (00–23).
	mm The minute (00–59).
	YY The year (00–99) (optional)
+format	Controls how the date is displayed. format is made up of a percent sign (%) followed by any of the following:
	n Inserts a newline
	t Inserts a tab
	m Month (digits)
	d Day of month (digits)
	y Last two digits of year
	D Date as mm/dd/yy

(continues)

Argument or Option	Description
H	Hour(00 - 23)
M	Minute
S	Second
I	Hour in 12-hour clock (01 - 12)
j	Julian date (001-366)
w	Day of week (0-6, 0=Sunday)
a	Sun, Mon, Tue, etc.
A	Full weekday name
h	Jan, Feb, Mar, etc.
B	Full month name
r	AM/PM notation for time.

Messages

```
no permission
```

or

```
UX:date: error: not privileged
```

You aren't the super user, and you tried to set the system date. The second message is from UnixWare.

```
bad conversion
```

You didn't give the date setting syntax correctly.

```
bad format character
```

You didn't use a format character from the preceding table.

Examples

```
date 0101130091
```

Sets the date and time to 01/01/91 at 1:00 p.m.

If you type in this command:

```
date "+Date = %D  Time = %H:%M"
```

this is the result:

```
Date = 01/01/91  Time = 13:00
```

dc

The desk calculator uses postfix notation (also referred to as reverse polish notation). If you aren't familiar with this format, use the bc command.

Syntax

```
dc progfile
```

Argument or Option	Description
progfile	An optional file name containing a set of dc commands.

Messages

```
O is unimplemented
```

O is replaced with the octal number of the character you type in. This means the character you type has no meaning in dc.

```
stack empty
```

The stack is empty; you didn't push enough arguments to perform the task.

Example

```
4 5 + p
```

This adds 4 and 5 and prints the result.

See also

bc

dd

dd stands for data dump, or device dump. It is useful for copying blocks of data to and from devices. It behaves differently than cp in that it can access the raw devices, for example, floppy drives. You can also use it to convert files so that they are suitable for a different platform of hardware.

For example, the swap argument allows you to swap each byte as it comes through dd. This is useful when migrating from a big-endian machine to a little-endian machine. Archiving programs such as tar write header information in native binary form to the devices they write to. A tar archive created on a Motorola-based machine is not normally readable on an Intel-based machine. By using dd in a pipeline and swapping the bytes, you can exchange tar files across platforms.

Syntax

```
dd [flag=value ] ...
```

Flags

Argument or Option	Description
if=file	Sets the input file, where file is the file name dd is to read. If this option is left blank dd reads from the standard input.

Argument or Option	Description
of=*file*	Sets the output file, where *file* is the file name to which dd is to write. If this option is left blank, dd writes to the standard output.
ibs=*input_buffer*	Sets the read buffer to the size of *input_buffer*. The default buffer size is BSIZE.
obs=*output_buffer*	Sets the write buffer to the size of *output_buffer*. The default buffer size is BSIZE.
bs=*i/o_buffer*	Sets both the read and the write buffer to the size of *i/o_buffer*. The default buffer size is BSIZE.
cbs=*conv_buffer*	Sets the conversion buffer to *conv_buffer*. This option is only valid with the conversion types of ascii, ebcdic, or ibm.
skip=*records*	Specifies the number of records to skip, before any output takes place. The record length is set by the ibs or bs arguments.
seek=*records*	Similar to skip but applies to the output file. dd seeks past existing records before it starts to copy.
iseek=*records*	Similar to skip except the input records are seeked past and not read (the iseek(S) routine is used).
files=*file_cnt*	Sets the number of input files to be considered as one file. When *file_count* EOFs are encountered the EOFs are ignored. (This option is useful only when reading from tape or floppy devices, as multiple EOFs may be on a tape.)
count=*records*	Copies only the number of records specified.

(continues)

Argument or Option	Description
conv=*conv_type*	Specifies the type of conversion. Valid types of conversions are:

	block	ASCII to unblocked ASCII
	unblock	unblocked ASCII to blocked
	ascii	EBCDIC to ASCII
	ebcdic	ASCII to EBCDIC
	ibm	Slightly different map then ebcdic
	lcase	To lowercase (if alphabetic)
	ucase	To uppercase (if alphabetic)
	swab	Swaps each pair of bytes (reads two bytes and swaps them, then the next two, and so on.)
	noerror	Continues to process even if an error is encountered.
	sync	Pads each input record to the length of ibs or bs.

Conversion types may be strung together separated by commas.

Rules

The numeric arguments: *input_buffer*, *output_buffer*, *i/o_buffer*, *file_cnt*, *records*, and *conv_buffer* may be followed by a modifier to specify the unit measures, as follows:

k	kilobytes
b	512 byte blocks
wa	word (2 bytes)

These arguments may also be separated by an x to indicate multiplication and the product of the numbers is used as the argument.

Messages

    dd: bad arg qf=ben

You gave dd a flag it didn't understand. In this case it was the flag qf=ben; qf isn't one of the valid flags.

    dd: cannot open frank

You gave dd an input file that it can't find, or you don't have permissions to open. In this example, the file it can't find is frank.

    36+1 records in

    36+1 records out

Every successful dd command reports the number of records read (records in) and the number of records written (records out). In this case, 36 records plus 1 partial record are read and written.

Examples

Suppose you download a tar file from a bulletin board and you want that file on a flopy disk. You can try to extract the tar file and then use the tar command to get the files you extracted to the floppy disk, or you can use the tar command to get the original tar command file to the floppy. But neither of these ideas really works very well in practice. dd helps. Suppose the file you download is a SCSI device driver and the name you give it is scsi_drive.tar. To get this onto a floppy disk, enter the following:

```
dd if=scsi_driver.tar of=/dev/rfd096ds15 bs=10k
```

This begins dumping the file scsi_driver.tar to the floppy drive in 10k increments.

Also suppose that file is compressed and is called scsi_driver.Z. Use the following command:

```
zcat scsi_driver.Z ¦ dd of=/dev/rfd096ds15 bs=10k
```

The zcat utility uncompresses the file to standard output. The file is then piped to dd, which places the contents on the floppy disk.

If you want to copy a disk but only have one floppy drive, you can use the following command:

```
dd if=/dev/rfd096ds15 of=tmp.file bs=10k
```

This reads the floppy drive and creates a file called tmp.file. Now place the formatted blank destination disk in the drive and enter:

```
dd if=tmp.file of=/dev/rfd096ds15 bs=10k
```

This reads the file tmp.file and places it on the floppy drive.

See also

tar, cpio, cp, copy, hd

deassign

See assign.

devnm

Reports the name of the directory's file system.

Syntax

    /etc/devnm dirname

Argument or Option	Description
dirname	The name of the directory you want reported and what file system name it resides in.

Example

    /etc/devnm /

Reports the following: root /.

df

Reports the amount of free disk space.

Syntax

    df [flags] filesystems

Argument or Option	Description
filesystems	This is an optional list of file systems from which to report the amount of free disk space. If this is left blank, all currently mounted file systems are reported.

Flags

Argument or Option	Description
-t	Normally df only reports the free space. With this option set, the total allocated size of the file system is reported, as well.
-f	With this flag set, df actually counts the number of free blocks instead of reading the number from the mount table (may not be available on all implementations of UNIX).
-v	This causes df to report the percentage free and the number of blocks.

Notes

df reports in blocks rather than bytes. Blocks are typically 512 bytes each; consult your system documentation for more information.

The -v option cannot be used with the other options.

Message

```
df: illegal arg badarg
```

You specified an option listed previously; *badarg* is replaced by the bad option you supplied.

See also

du, mount

diff

Compares two text files, and reports what must be done to the one to make it look like the other. diff also can be used to create a script usable by the editor ed to re-create the second file from the first. To compare binary files use cmp.

Syntax

    diff [flags] oldfile newfile

Argument or Option	Description
oldfile	This is the file that you want diff to compare and then report what has to be done to it to make it look like newfile.
newfile	This is the name of the file you want to use to compare to oldfile. In a sense this is the control file, as diff reports what it takes to make oldfile look like newfile.

Flags

Argument or Option	Description
-b	Causes leading and trailing blanks and tabs to compare as equal. (For example, "the big tree" is the same as "the big tree.")
-e	Generates a script suitable for the editor ed.
-f	Similar to the -e flag, this producesa script in the opposite order. However, this is not usable by ed.

Notes

The output of diff takes any one of the following forms
where each form shows a line number range and the text
being referenced after:

```
lineno a from-lineno to-lineno
```

The text in the first file lineno has to have the text in the
second file from-lineno to the to-lineno added to it. The text
found in the second file is shown preceded by a greater than
sign (>). This shows that these lines were only found in the
second file.

```
from-lineno to-lineno d lineno
```

The text in the first file found at line number from-lineno to
the line number to-lineno must be deleted. If these lines
were to exist they would fall after the line number in the
second file lineno. The text to be deleted follows and is preceded by a less than sign (<). This shows that these lines are
only found in the first file.

```
from-lineno to-lineno c from-lineno to-lineno
```

In this line diff shows how two sets of lines are different and
have to be changed from the first set of line number ranges
to match the second set of line number ranges. The text that
has to be changed follows and is preceded by <. The text, as
found in the second file, follows this and is preceded by >.

Example

```
diff old-letter letter-to-dad
```

Change the file old-letter so it looks like the file letter-
to -dad.

See also

ed

diff3

Compares three files at once.

Syntax

```
diff3 [flags] file1 file2 file3
```

Argument or Option	Description
file1	The first file used in the comparison, probably the older of the three.
file2	The second file used in the comparison.
file3	The third file used in the comparison.

Flags

Argument or Option	Description
-e	Produces a script for ed to change file1 to reflect the differences between file2 and file3.
-x	Produces a script for ed to change file1 to reflect the differences in all files.
-3	Produces a script for ed to change file1 to reflect the differences in file3.

Example

```
diff3 old-letter letter-to-mom new-letter
```

Compares the three letters and displays the results of the comparison.

See also

diff, comm, cmp, ed, sdiff

dircmp

Compares the contents of two directories listing which files only are found in one or the other, and runs diff on each of the files sharing the same name.

Syntax

```
dircmp [flags] dir1 dir2
```

Argument or Option	Description
dir1	The name of the directory to use in the comparison. A period (.) means the current directory.
dir2	The name of the second directory, also can be a period (.).

Flags

Argument or Option	Description
-d	Runs a "full" diff on the files named the same. Normally, dircmp just reports if the contents are the same or not.
-s	Suppresses the displaying of identical file names in both directories.

Argument or Option	Description
-w*width*	Sets the width of the output to *width* characters; the default is 72.

Example

```
dircmp /usr/bin /bin
```

Compares the two executable paths /usr/bin and /bin.

See also

diff

dirname

Enables you to extract the directory portion of a path name. This is useful in shell scripts.

Syntax

```
dirname pathname
```

Argument or Option	Description
pathname	The path name for which you want to know the directory portion. If no slashes (/) are used in the string provided, then a period (.) is returned.

Examples

```
dirname /usr/bin/test
```

The result displayed on-screen is /usr/bin.

```
dirname /usr/bin
```

Results in /usr. Even though bin is a directory, dirname doesn't look at the file system to determine what the directory portion of the string is; it just looks for the last slash, and assumes everything before that.

```
dirname usr
```

The result written to standard output is a period (.).

See also

basename, sh

disable

You use disable to disallow terminals to be logged on to the printer or print jobs to be applied to the printer. When you disable a printer, jobs may still be queued for that printer; however, the jobs are not completed on the printer. This is useful when clearing up paper jams or temporarily replacing the printer for servicing.

Syntax

```
disable terminals

disable -c -rreason printers
```

Argument or Option	Description
terminals	The list of terminals you wish to disable. These terminals will no longer accept logins.
-c	Use this flag when you wish to cancel the job that is currently printing.

Argument or Option	Description
-r*reason*	If the printer will be disabled for an extended period of time, you may want to tell the users. *reason* must immediately follow -r, and if it is more than one word, enclose it in quotation marks (").
printers	The list of printers to disable.

Note

When you disable a printer, the print job currently printing is stopped. When you enable the printer again, this job starts from the beginning, unless you used the -c flag.

Examples

```
disable tty12
```

Disables the twelfth console terminal.

```
disable frontdsk
```

Disables the printer called frontdsk.

```
disable -c -r"servicing, back up in 1 hr." frontdsk
```

Disables the frontdsk printer, cancels the currently printing job, and notifies users checking on the status of this printer why it is disabled and when it will be back in service.

See also

enable, cancel, lp, lpstat

diskcmp

See diskcp.

diskcp

diskcp copies floppy disks and diskcmp compares the contents of floppy disks using cmp. You can make multiple copies of a single floppy disk or multiple copies of multiple source floppy disks. Both diskcp and diskcmp contain self-explanatory prompts for their use.

Syntax

```
diskcp [flags]
diskcmp [flags]
```

Flags

Argument or Option	Description
-f	Format the target floppy before copying; only valid with diskcp.
-d	If you have a dual-drive machine, the floppy disks are copied or compared directly; normally a copy of the source floppy is copied to the hard disk.
-s	This flag uses sum to run a check sum on the copy to verify the accuracy of the copy.
-48ds9	Specifies the 360K floppy.
-96ds9	Specifies the 720K 5 1/4-inch floppy.

Argument or Option	Description
-96ds15	Specifies the 1.2M floppy.
-135ds9	Specifies the 720K 3 1/2-inch floppy.
-135ds18	Specifies the 1.44M floppy.

Rule

These utilities work with two floppy disks when both floppy disks are the same density. When you have a 3 1/2-inch and a 5 1/4-inch drive, these utilities work only with the primary drive. Because both utilities are shell scripts, it is possible to modify them to accommodate the secondary drive.

Example

```
diskcp -s -135ds18
```

Copies a 3 1/2-inch floppy and runs a checksum to verify the copy.

See also

dd, cmp, sum, format

doscat

Enables you to mimic the UNIX cat utility on a DOS disk or partition.

Syntax

```
doscat -r -m filelist
```

Argument or Option	Description
-r	Specifies a raw copy; no newline translation occurs. (See the "Rules" section for a definition of newline translation.) When copying binary files, such as word processing, spreadsheets, and database files, use this option.
-m	Forces newline translation. Normally, the DOS utilities test to see if newline translations should be done. If the utilities can't determine this, -m forces newline translation.
filelist	The list of files you want to copy to standard output. File names consist of a drive specification followed by the directory specification. Although you access DOS files, use UNIX conventions; don't use backslashes. You may also use drive letters, as defined in the /etc /default/msdos file. This file is a map of drive letters to UNIX devices, and enables you to use familiar DOS convention drive specifications. (For example, a:letter.mom.)

Rules

Newline translation involves the conversion of the way DOS stores text files and UNIX stores text files. DOS uses a carriage return and a line-feed character to signify the end of a line. It also uses Ctrl-Z to signify the end of a file. UNIX uses one line-feed character, referred to as the *newline character,* and no end-of-file marker.

The -r and -m options cannot be used together.

Examples

```
doscat /dev/rfd096:letter.mom
```

Copies the file letter.mom found on the DOS disk in the
primary high-density drive.

```
doscat a:letter.mom
```

This is similar to the previous example except that it uses the
/etc/default/msdos file to map a to a UNIX device.

See also

cat, doscp, dosdir, dosformat, dosls, dosmkdir, dosrm,
dosrmdir, xtod, dtox

doscp

Enables you to mimic the UNIX cp utility on a DOS disk or
partition.

Syntax

```
doscp -r -m filelist dir
doscp -r -m source dest
```

Argument or Option	Description
-r	Specifies a raw copy, that is, no newline translation is to occur. (See the discussion in the "Rules" section for a definition of newline translation.) When copying binary files, such as word processing, spreadsheets, and database files, this option should be used.

(continues)

Argument or Option	Description
-m	Forces newline translation. Normally, the DOS utilities test to see if newline translation should be done. This option forces it to be true if the utilities can't determine if it should be done.
filelist	This is the list of files you want to copy. File names consist of a drive specification followed by the directory specification. Although you are accessing DOS files, UNIX conventions are used; don't use backslashes. You may also use drive letters as defined in the /etc/default/msdos file. This file is a map of drive letters to UNIX devices, thus allowing you to use familiar DOS convention drive specifications (for example, a:letter.mom).
dir	The directory for the list of files to be copied to.
source	The source file name to be copied.
dest	The destination file name of the copy.

Rules

Newline translation involves the conversion of the way DOS stores text files and UNIX stores text files. DOS uses a carriage return and a line-feed character to signify the end of a line. It also uses a Ctrl-Z to signify the end of a file. UNIX uses one line-feed character, referred to as the newline character, and no end-of-file marker.

The -r and -m options may not be used together.

Examples

```
doscp /dev/rfd096:letter.mom letter-to-mom
```

Copies the file letter.mom found on the DOS disk in the
primary high-density drive.

```
doscp a:letter.mom letter-to-mom
```

This is similar to the previous example except that it uses the
/etc/default/msdos file to map a to a UNIX device.

See also

cat, doscat, dosdir, dosformat, dosls, dosmkdir, dosrm,
dosrmdir, xtod, dtox

dosdir

dosdir produces a directory listing similar to that of the DOS
command DIR.

Syntax

```
dosdir drive
```

Argument or Option	Description
drive	The drive for which you want a directory listing. You can use the DOS convention or the UNIX device name.

Examples

```
dosdir a:
```

Gives a DOS style listing of the floppy disk found in the a:
drive as defined by the /etc/default/msdos file.

```
dosdir /dev/rfd096
```

This is similar to the previous command, but uses the UNIX device name.

See also

ls, doscat, doscp, dosformat, dosmkdir, dosls, dosrm, dosrmdir

dosformat

Creates DOS 2.0 formatted disks.

Syntax

```
dosformat [flags] drive
```

Argument or Option	Description
drive	The drive to be formatted. You can use the DOS convention or the UNIX device name.

Flags

Argument or Option	Description
-f	Suppresses the interactive nature of dosformat.
-q	Specifies quiet operation and suppresses the messages normally displayed while using dosformat.
-v	Specifies a volume label of as many as 11 characters.

Rule

You cannot use dosformat to format a hard disk.

Examples

    dosformat /dev/rfd096

Formats the high-density drive.

    dosformat a:

Formats the drive mapped to a: in the /etc/default/msdos file.

See also

format, doscat, doscp, dosdir, dosmkdir, dosls, dosrm, dosrmdir

dosls

Produces a directory list of the contents of the DOS floppy or hard disk partition; has the format of ls.

Syntax

    dosls drive

Argument or Option	Description
drive	The drive for which you want a directory listing. You can use the DOS convention or the UNIX device name.

Examples

```
dosls a:
```

Gives an ls style listing of the floppy found in the a: drive as defined by the /etc/default/msdos file.

```
dosls /dev/rfd096
```

This is similar to the previous command, but uses the UNIX device name.

See also

ls, doscat, doscp, dosdir, dosformat, dosmkdir, dosrm, dosrmdir

dosmkdir

This allows you to make a directory on the DOS floppy or partition.

Syntax

```
dosmkdir directory
```

Argument or Option	Description
directory	The directory you want to create. Directory names consist of a drive specification followed by the directory specification. Although you access DOS files, use UNIX conventions; don't use backslashes(\). You can use drive letters as defined in the /etc /default/msdos file. This file is a map of drive letters to UNIX devices, and enables you to use familiar DOS convention drive specifications. (For example, a:letter.mom.)

Examples

```
dosmkdir /dev/rfd096:/letters
```

Creates the directory /letters found on the DOS disk in the primary high-density drive.

```
dosmkdir a:/letters
```

This is similar to the previous example except that it uses the /etc/default/msdos file to map a: to a UNIX device.

See also

mkdir, doscat, doscp, dosdir, dosformat, dosls, dosrm, dosrmdir

dosrm

Enables you to remove files found on the DOS floppy or partition. dosrm mimics the rm command.

Syntax

```
dosrm filelist
```

Argument or Option	Description
filelist	The list of files you want to delete. File names consist of a drive specification followed by the directory specification. Although you access DOS files, use UNIX conventions; don't use back-slashes(\). You can use drive letters as defined in the /etc/default /msdos file. This file is a map of drive letters to UNIX devices, and enables you to use familiar DOS convention drive specifications. (For example, a:letter.mom.)

Examples

    dosrm /dev/rfd096:letter.mom

Deletes the file letter.mom found on the DOS disk in the primary high-density drive.

    dosrm a:letter.mom

This is similar to the previous example except that it uses the /etc/default/msdos file to map a: to a UNIX device.

See also

doscat, doscp, dosdir, dosformat, dosls, dosmkdir, dosrmdir

dosrmdir

Enables you to remove a directory on the DOS floppy or partition.

Syntax

    dosrmdir *directory*

Argument or Option	Description
directory	The directory you want to remove. Directory names consist of a drive specification followed by the directory specification. Although you access DOS files, use UNIX conventions; don't use back-slashes(\). You can use drive letters as defined in the /etc/default /msdos file. This file is a map of drive letters to UNIX devices, and enables you to use familiar DOS convention drive specifications (for example, a:letter.mom).

Examples

```
dosrmdir /dev/rfd096:/letters
```

Removes the directory /letters found on the DOS disk in
the primary high-density drive.

```
dosrmdir a:/letters
```

This is similar to the previous example except that it uses the
/etc/default/msdos file to map a: to a UNIX device.

See also

rmdir, doscat, doscp, dosdir, dosformat, dosls, dosrm,
dosmkdir

dtox

Converts DOS text files to UNIX text files. UNIX uses one
character to mean the end of a line: the newline or linefeed
character. Whereas DOS uses two: a linefeed and a carriage
return. Furthermore, DOS has an end-of-file marker (Ctrl-Z).
Without running a conversion on the files, UNIX does not
understand the format of the files you create. Do not use
dtox on binary/data files.

Syntax

```
dtox dos-filename
```

Argument or Option	Description
dos-filename	The name of the DOS file you want to convert to UNIX format. If left blank, dtox reads from standard input. dtox always writes to standard output.

Example

```
dtox dosletter >letter-to-mom
```

Converts the file `dosletter`; places the results into a file
called `letter-to-mom`.

See also

xtod, doscp

dtype

Provides information about the format of your specified disk
and presents an exit code from the following table.

Exit Code	Message
60	Error
61	Empty or unrecognized data
70	Backup format, volume n
71	tar format (,extent e of n)
72	cpio format
73	cpio character format
80	DOS 1.x, 8 sec/track, single-sided
81	DOS 1.x, 8 sec/track, double-sided
90	DOS 2.x, 8 sec/track, single-sided
91	DOS 2.x, 8 sec/track, double-sided
92	DOS 2.x, 9 sec/track, single-sided
93	DOS 2.x, 9 sec/track, double-sided
94	DOS 2.x, fixed disk

Exit Code	Message
110	DOS 3.x, 9 sec/track, double-sided
120	XENIX 2.x file system (needs cleaning)
130	XENIX 3.x file system (needs cleaning)
140	UNIX 1K file system (needs cleaning)

Syntax

```
dtype -s devices
```

Argument or Option	Description
-s	The messages are not displayed, only the exit status is used. The exit status is valid for the last device.
devices	List of devices to check the format in which the media is stored.

Rule

This command is only reliable on floppy disks. The tar, cpio, and backup formats may not be recognizable if created on a foreign system.

Message

```
/usr/bin   : unrecognized data
```

Asks for the disk type of the directory /usr/bin. Because /usr/bin isn't a device, dtype gives this message.

Example

```
dtype /dev/rfd096
```

Reports what kind of format is used on the floppy disk in the primary high-density drive.

du

du displays the amount of space used by the specified directories or files. The information is reported in 512 byte blocks.

Syntax

```
du [flags] names
```

Argument or Option	Description
names	The list of directories or files for which you want to have the space requirements calculated. If left blank, the current directory is used.

Flags

Argument or Option	Description
-s	Causes only a total for each of the specified names. Normally, a number for every subdirectory is displayed.
-a	Causes each file encountered to be displayed with its size.
-f	Only the directories in the currently mounted file system are traversed; other file systems are ignored. May not be supported on some implementations of UNIX.

Argument or Option	Description
-u	Causes files with more than one link to be ignored. May not be supported on some implementations of UNIX.
-r	Produces a message if the directory can't be read.

Note

Files with more than one link are only counted once. However, du has a maximum number of links it can table; when this maximum is exceeded, the sizes used by these files are included in the total.

Examples

```
du -s /usr/bin /bin
```

Reports the total space in 512 byte blocks used by the two directories /usr/bin and /bin.

```
du
```

Reports the space usage of the current directory and gives a number for each subdirectory encountered.

See also

df

echo

This command takes the arguments passed to it and writes them to standard output. echo is useful in shell scripts to prompt for input or to report the status of a process.

Syntax

```
echo -n string
```

Argument or Option	Description
-n	Normally, echo follows all the output with a newline; this option suppresses that.
string	The string of characters you wish to output. The following special characters produce special output sequences:

Sequence	Meaning
\b	Backspace
\c	Don't print a newline at the end
\f	Formfeed
\n	Newline
\r	Carriage return
\t	Tab
\v	Vertical tab
\\	Backslash
\0n	n is a 1-, 2-, or 3-digit octal number, representing a character.

Examples

```
echo Hello
```

Prints Hello on the standard output.

```
echo "enter Y or N \c"
```

Prompts the user for a Y or N response without echoing a newline.

```
echo
```

Produces a newline.

```
echo 'Can you hear this \07\07\07?'
```

Demonstrates the use of the octal digits. Here it is used to sound the terminal bell three times.

See also

sh, cat

ed

A line editor that is useful on systems or terminals that don't support full screen editors, such as vi. ed, that also can be used to edit files in batch by created ed scripts.

Syntax

```
ed - -p prompt filename
```

Argument or Option	Description
-	Suppresses the messages produced by the e, r, w, q, and ! commands.
-p prompt	Enables you specify your own prompt string.

(continues)

Argument or Option	Description
filename	The name of the file you want to edit. You edit only one file at a time.

Note

ed is rather complex and powerful. For more information, see the user's guide and reference provided with your system, or use a book dedicated to the usage of ed.

Example

```
ed letter-to-dad
```

Starts ed to edit letter-to-dad.

See also

vi, ex, sed

egrep

See grep.

enable

Allows terminals to be logged on to the printer and print jobs to be applied to the printer.

Syntax

```
enable terminals

enable printers
```

Argument or Option	Description
`terminals`	A list of terminals to enable. These terminals accept logins.
`printers`	A list of printers to enable.

Examples

```
enable tty12
```

Enables the twelfth console terminal.

```
enable frontdsk
```

Enables the printer called `frontdsk`.

See also

disable, cancel, lp, lpstat

env

Modifies the environment for the execution of a command without affecting the current environment. It also can be used to display the current environment.

Syntax

```
env - name=value command
```

Argument or Option	Description
-	Restricts the environment to only those values to follow in the `name=value` list. Normally, env adds the list to environment.

(continues)

Argument or Option	Description
name=value	Allows you to pass environment variables to the command specifying the value of the variable for this execution of the command. You may pass multiple variables simply by repeating the name=value format.
command	The name of the command and its arguments to be run with the specified environment.

Examples

```
env
```

Prints the current environment in a *name=value* format, one per line.

```
env HOME=/usr/sue sh
```

Runs a new shell with the home directory set up as /usr/sue.

expr

Enables you to evaluate expressions in shell scripts. These expressions can be mathematical or string oriented. String functions include returning substrings, length of a string, and more.

Syntax

```
expr arguments
```

Arguments

Argument or Option	Description
arg1 ¦ arg2	arg1 is evaluated, and if it is neither null or 0, it is returned; otherwise, arg2 is evaluated and returned.
arg1 & arg2	Both arg1 and arg2 are evaluated and if neither one is null or 0, arg1 is returned; otherwise, 0 is returned.
arg1 { =, ==, >, >=, <, <=, != } arg2	arg1 is compared to arg2 using any of the logical operators; = and == are functionally equivalent. If both arg1 and arg2 are integers, then the comparison is numeric. If either is a string, then the comparison is done lexicographically as defined by the locale; typically, this means an ASCII comparison (for example, "cat" is greater than "car," and "bat" is less than "cat"). If the comparison is true, then the result is a 1; otherwise, the result is a 0.
arg1 { *, /, % } arg2	Multiplication, division, or modulo of arg1 and arg2.
arg1 { +, - } arg2	Addition or subtraction of arg1 and arg2.
string : match_expr	The colon (:) is a matching operator. string is compared to the expression match_expr. The result of the command is the match, based on match_expr. match_expr is any regular expression (one exemption is that all expressions are considered to be "anchored" as if a caret (^) had been used). Normally the

(continues)

Argument or Option	Description
	result of the matching operator is the number of characters that match. You can use the notation \(*reg_expr* \) to return a substring.
match *string match_expr*	Same as *string* : *match_expr* but different syntax.
substr *string beg_pos len*	Returns a substring of *string* beginning at position *beg_pos* for length of *len* characters. expr counts *beg_pos* characters from the beginning of the string *string* and returns each character after that for *len* characters. *beg_pos* must be an integer greater than zero. *len* must be a positive integer.
length *string*	Returns the length of the string *string*. That is, expr counts the number of characters in the string.
index *string char_set*	Returns the location of *char_set* in the string *string*. Typically *char_set* is one character and expr returns the offset location of that character in the string. If *char_set* is several characters, expr returns the offset location of the first character in the set it finds in the string. If *char_set* is not in the string, a 0 is returned.

Rules

Each argument presented to expr must be separated by spaces. All characters that are also special to the shell must be escaped. The output of expr is the standard output. Integers are treated internally as 32 bit 2's compliment numbers. Parentheses () may be used for grouping.

The exit status may be any of the following:

Argument or Option	Description
0	The expression is neither null nor 0.
1	The expression is null or 0.
2	An invalid expression is encountered.

expr recognizes operators only by their values, not their position, so it is possible for expr to have a problem after the shell expands the arguments given to it. For example, in the following expr statement.

```
a="="; b="="# assign the variables a & b the equal sign
"="xpr $a = $b
```

What expr sees is:

```
expr = = =
```

expr thinks it has a bad expression because its first argument is an equal sign (=). The following code segment allows for the comparison of equal signs.

```
expr X$a = X$b
```

which after substitution looks like:

```
expr X= = X=
```

Messages

```
syntax error
```

You used an invalid operator, or referenced a variable and did not set it.

```
nonnumeric argument
```

You attempted an arithmetic function and used an argument that is not numeric.

Examples

When writing a shell script, you need to be able to iterate until you reach a certain limit. Suppose you want to allow the user to pick how many times the date appears on-screen. To do this, you can code the following shell script:

```
echo "Enter number of dates to display \c"
read DATE_CNT
i=0
while ($i < $DATE_CNT)
do
date
i='expr $i + 1'
done
```

With expr, you can mimic the function of the basename command with the following:

```
:
# argument passed is the file name to get the basename of.

expr $1 : '.*/\(.*\)'
```

This example is more complicated and not as intuitive as the date displayed on-screen example. If you look at this example more closely, you see that the matching operator : is used and that it compares what is passed, $1, with the expression .*/\(.*\).

Item	Description
.*	A regular expression that matches zero or more occurrences of any character.
/	A single character regular expression matching itself, a slash /.

Item	Description
\(.*\)	The .* is a regular expression matching zero or more occurrences of any character. The \(\) notation causes these "zero or more occurrences of any character" to result in expr.

You read this regular expression as "return the set of characters that follow a slash preceded by any number of other characters or no characters."

See also

awk, basename, bc, dc, sh

fgrep

See grep.

file

Determines the type of a file. file is able to recognize whether the file is 386 executable, 286 executable, command text, ASCII text, C source, and so on. Many of the UNIX commands are only shell scripts. file can be used to report to you which ones are and which ones are not scripts. It also is useful to determine if the file is "text" based or not and whether it can be viewed or edited.

Syntax

```
file [ -f ffile ] filelist
```

Argument or Option	Description
-f *ffile*	Tells file that the list of files to identify is found in *ffile*. This is useful when many files must be identified.
filelist	A space separated list of files of or about which you want to know the type.

Messages

```
filename: cannot open
```

You asked file to type a file that doesn't exist; *filename* is replaced by the file you requested.

```
filename: cannot open for reading
```

The file you requested exists, but you don't have read permissions; *filename* is replaced by the file you requested.

Example

```
file /unix
```

Examines the file /unix and reports what type of file it is.

See also

The internal type command of sh.

find

find is an extremely powerful tool. It traverses the specified directories generating a list of files that match the criteria specified. Files may be matched by name, size, creation time, modification time, and many more critieria. You even can execute a command on the matched files each time a file is found.

Syntax

```
find dirlist match-spec
```

Argument or Option	Description
`dirlist`	A space separated list of the directories in which you want to look for a file or set of files.
`match-spec`	The matching specification or description of files you want to find. See the "Flags" section for a list of possible `match-spec` values.

Flags

Argument or Option	Description
`-name file`	Tells find what file to search for. If enclosed in quotation marks (") `file` can contain wild cards (* and ?).
`-perm mode`	Matches all files whose mode matches the numeric value of `mode`. All modes must be matched—not just read, write, and execute. If preceded by a negative (-), `mode` takes on the meaning of everything without this mode.
`-type c`	Matches all files whose type is listed in the following table:

c	Character device
b	Block special
d	Directory
p	Named pipe
f	Regular file (not c, b, d, or p)

(continues)

Argument or Option	Description
`-links` *n*	Matches all files with *n* number of links.
`-size` *n*	Matches all files of size *n* blocks (512 byte blocks). If *n* is preceded by a +, matches all files larger than *n* blocks. If *n* is preceded by a -, matches those less than *n* blocks.
`-user` *user-id*	Matches all files whose user id is *user-id*. May either be the numeric value or the logname of the user.
`-atime` *n*	Matches all files last accessed within the previous *n* days.
`-mtime` *n*	Matches all files modified within the previous *n* days.
`-exec` *cmd*	For each file matched, the command *cmd* is executed. The notation {} is used to signify where the file name should appear in the command executed. The command must be terminated by an escaped semicolon (\;), for example, `-exec ls -d {} \;` Here the command `ls` is executed with the `-d` argument, and each file is passed to `ls` at the place where the {} is found.
`-ok` *cmd*	Same as `-exec` except the user is prompted for confirmation before the command is executed.
`-newer` *file*	Matches all files that have been modified more recently than *file*.

Notes

The expressions (flags) may be grouped together and combined to limit the search criteria. Multiple flags are assumed to be ANDs. Both criteria must be met. To offer more control over selection, the following table describes other options:

Argument or Option	Description
( )	Parentheses can be used to group selections. Because the parentheses are special to the shell, they must be escaped (\ ( )).
-o	This is the OR operator that overrides the default AND assumption.
!	This is a NOT operator that negates the expression that follows it.
+ -	The *n* arguments may be preceded by a plus (+) or a negative (-) to denote either more than or less than, respectively.

Messages

```
find: bad option -badoption
```

A *match-spec* that is not valid was used. *badoption* is replaced with what was specified.

```
find: incomplete statement
```

find did not have enough arguments for it to understand what you wanted.

Examples

```
find . -name letter-to-dad -print
```

Searches the current directory and its subdirectories for a file called letter-to-dad. When, and if it finds it, the full path name is shown on-screen.

```
find . -name "letter*" -print
```

Looks for all files starting with letter. Note the use of the wild card (*). This allows for a pattern match of all files starting with the characters letter. This finds: letters, letter_to_dad, letter_to_mom, and so on.

```
find . -name "letter*" -exec ls -l {} \;
```

This example searches for the files starting with `letter` and executes a long listing on them. Notice the placement of the `{}` and the escaped semicolon `\;`.

```
find . ! \( -name "letter*" -o -name "*dad" \) -
print
```

This example is more complicated. This command looks for a list of files that doesn't start with `letter` or end with `dad`.

finger

Displays information about users on the system.

Syntax

```
finger [flags] users
```

Argument or Option	Description
users	This is an optional list of user names. If specified, then extended information about the user is displayed.

Flags

Argument or Option	Description
-b	Displays a briefer output
-f	Suppresses header lines
-i	Displays a quick list with idle times
-l	Forces the long (extended) output
-p	Doesn't print the .plan file
-q	Displays a quick list of users

Rules

Finger reads the information in the comment field of the
/etc/passwd file. The comment field is divided into three
subfields, each separated by a comma. The second field requires two commas. For example, if the comment field contains Frank Burns, Swamp, Mash, 555-2939, then Frank Burns is
displayed under "In real life," Swamp, Mash under "office," and
555-2939 under "home phone."

The extended information about users includes the comment
field described previously and two files found in their home
directories (.plan and .project). The contents of these files
are displayed on-screen.

Idle time is the time elapsed since something displayed
on-screen or the user typed something. This is not true idle
time, as it is possible for a program to do useful work without
requiring the user's intervention.

An asterisk(*) before the terminal name indicates that the
user does not give others write permission.

Examples

    finger

Lists all users on the system.

    finger frank susie

Lists extended information about frank and susie.

See also

    who, w

format

Formats floppy disks for use with UNIX. UNIX requires perfect media on floppy disks; it can't deal with bad spots on a floppy disk. format verifies the disk to make sure it is writeable and readable.

Syntax

format *device*

Argument or Option	Description
device	The name of the raw device you want to format (for example, /dev/rdsk/5h is the primary 5 1/4-inch high-density drive)
-v	Verbose
-V	Verify with one random write/read/compare
-E	Exhaustive verify where every track is write/read/compare

Note

format prompts you to enter the floppy disk when ready, however; format does not prompt you to format another. You have to reinvoke the format command.

Examples

format /dev/rdsk/5h

Formats a 5 1/4-inch high-density disk.

format /dev/rdsk/3h

Formats a 3 1/2-inch high-density disk.

grep

grep looks for patterns found in files and reports to you when these patterns are found. The name of the command comes from the use of "regular expressions" in the ed family of editors. grep stands for "Global Regular Express Printer."

Syntax

```
grep [flags] reg-expres filelist

egrep [flags] reg-expres filelist

fgrep [flags] string filelist
```

Argument or Option	Description
filelist	An optional space separated list of files to search for the given string or reg-expres. If left blank, the standard input is searched.
reg-expres	The regular expression to search for. Regular expressions are in the form used by ed. See the man page for the definition of regular expressions.
string	The string you want to find in the files.

Flags

Argument or Option	Description
-v	Lists the lines that don't match string or reg-expres.
-c	Counts the matching lines.
-l	Only the file names containing a match are displayed.

(continues)

Argument or Option	Description
-h	Suppresses the name of the file in which the match was found from being displayed (grep and egrep only).
-n	Each matching line is displayed along with its relative line number.
-i	Causes matching to not be case-sensitive. The default behavior is case-sensitive.
-e reg-expres	Useful when the regular expression or string starts with a dash(-).
-f file	file contains the strings or expressions to search for.

Notes

fgrep stands for fast grep and can only search for fixed strings. Multiple strings may be searched for by separating each string by a newline or by entering them in the -f file file.

egrep stands for extended grep and accepts the following enhancements to regular expressions defined by ed.

+	If this trails a regular expression it matches one or more of that occurrence.
?	If this trails a regular expression it matches 0 or 1 occurrences.
|	Used to denote multiple regular expressions (for example, this or that expression).
( )	May be used to group expressions.

Messages

```
grep: illegal option -- badoption
```

You gave grep an option/flag that it doesn't understand; *badoption* is replaced by the option specified.

```
grep: can't open file
```

You tried to search a file that doesn't exist or for which you don't have read permissions; *file* is replaced by the file you specified.

Examples

```
grep hello letter-to-dad
```

Searches for the word hello in the file letter-to-dad.

```
fgrep hello letter-to-dad
```

This does the same thing.

```
grep "[hH]ello" letter-to-dad
```

Searches for the word hello or Hello.

```
fgrep "hello
Hello" letter-to-dad
```

This does the same thing.

```
egrep "([Ss]ome¦[Aa]ny)one" letter-to-dad
```

Looks for all the words someone, Someone, anyone, or Anyone in the file.

```
vi 'fgrep -l hello *'
```

Generates a list of file names in the current directory that have the word hello in them and passes this list of names to the editor vi.

See also

sh, ed

hd

hexdump in Linux (handwritten)

hd stands for hex dump. Use hd to see the hexadecimal representations of the contents of a file. Viewers such as pg and more are designed for *text-based files*. These files consist of printable characters. *Binary files* are typically files generated by a database. Today, most spreadsheets and word-processing documents are also binary. There are times when you need to look at an area of a binary file and more doesn't work.

Syntax

```
hd [ -format ] [ -s offset ] [ -n count ] [ file-list ]
```

Flags

Argument or Option	Description
-format	Format specifies the behavior for generating the output. The default format is: -abxA (show addresses, use the bytes output format, the numeric base is hexadecimal, and shows the ASCII output on the right side). Formats can be combined to produce multiple output lines per 16 byte record.
	a Generates the address offset for each 16 byte record read, on the far left side of the output generated.
	c Shows all printable characters as themselves and nonprintable characters are shown in the chosen output base.
	b Shows input as bytes in the chosen output base—each 8 bits.

Argument or Option	Description		
	w		Shows input as a word in the chosen output base—each 16 bits.
	l		Shows input as a long in the chosen output base—each 32 bits.
	A		Shows printable characters as themselves and all others as a period (.). This is displayed on the right side of the output generated.
	What the number base of the output should be		
		x	The output uses hexadecimal as the base.
		d	The output uses decimal as the base.
		o	The output uses octal as the base.
-s *offset*	Specifies how many bytes (*offset*) to read (skip) from the input file before output starts. *offset* can be specified in decimal, octal, or hexadecimal. For example:		
	11		(decimal) skip 11 bytes
	013		(octal) skip 11(decimal) bytes
	0x0b		(hexadecimal) skip 11(decimal) bytes
	You can use the following modifiers to change the number's unit of measure:		
	w		words (2 bytes)
	l		long word (4 bytes)

(continues)

Argument or Option	Description
	b "blocks" (512 bytes)
	k kilobytes (1024 bytes)
	Because it is valid for a hexadecimal number to end in a b, you cannot use the preceding modifiers when specifying hexadecimal *offsets*. You may, however, use the asterisk (*) separated by a space to specify a multiplier (for example, 0x0b * 512).
-n *count*	Specifies the total number of bytes to process. *count* follows the same rules as *offset* for formatting.
file-list	The list of files to process, each separated by a space. If no file is specified, then the input is the standard input.

Messages

```
hd: cannot access ben.1
```

You attempted to dump a file that doesn't exist, in this example that file is ben.1.

```
0000    74 6f 74 61 6c 20 31 35  32 0a 2d 72 77 2d 72 77
   total 152.-rw-rw
0010    2d 72 77 2d 20 20 20 31  20 62 65 6e 61 68 20 20
   -rw-   1 benah
0020    20 20 70 72 6f 67 20 20  20 20 20 20 20 33 37 30
      prog          370
0030    32 31 20 46 65 62 20 31  32 20 31 37 3a 32 33 20
   21 Feb 12 17:23
0040    62 65 6e 0a 2d 72 77 2d  72 77 2d 72 77 2d 20 20
   ben.-rw-rw-rw-
```

```
0050      20 31 20 62 65 6e 61 68    20 20 20 20 70 72 6f 67
      1 benah        prog
0060      20 20 20 20 20 20 20 33    37 30 32 31 20 46 65 62
            37021 Feb
0070      20 31 32 20 31 37 3a 32    36 20 62 65 6e 32 0a 2d
      12 17:26 ben2.-
0080      72 77 2d 72 77 2d 72 77    2d 20 20 20 31 20 62 65
      rw-rw-rw-    1 be
0090      6e 61 68 20 20 20 20 70    72 6f 67 20 20 20 20 20
      nah    prog
00a0      20 20 20 20 20 20 30 20    46 65 62 20 31 32 20 31
            0 Feb 12 1
00b0      37 3a 32 38 20 62 65 6e    33 0a
      7:28 ben3.
00ba
```

This sample output uses the default *format*. Notice the address offsets on the left, the hexadecimal output of 16 bytes in the middle, and the ASCII output of those records on the right.

Examples

Suppose someone used a word processor or spreadsheet to create a very unusual file name on the system. This name is corrupt because, when you do a ls -C on the directory, everything is scrambled on-screen. You know that some sort of unprintable character was used but you don't know what it was. To figure this out, you can pass a directory listing through hd as in the following:

    ls ¦ hd

Produces a listing in hexadecimal form and enables you to see the nonprintable character's hexadecimal representation. You can then identify the faulty file name and remove it or rename it.

See also

od, ls, more, pg

head

head prints out the first number of specified lines of a file.

Syntax

head -*lines* *filelist*

Argument or Option	Description
-*lines*	The number of lines to print from the beginning of the file. The default is 10.
filelist	A space separated list of file names you want displayed. If left blank, the standard input is read.

Example

head letter-to-dad

Prints the first 10 lines from the file letter-to-dad.

See also

tail, pr, cat, more, pg

hello

hello sends messages to another terminal, if that terminal is set up to receive messages. This command functions in the same way as write, except that as each character is typed, it is sent to the user's terminal. This character-by-character transmission is unlike `write` which waits until a newline is encountered to transmit.

Syntax

```
hello user tty
```

Argument or Option	Description
user	The name of the user to whom you want to send a message.
tty	An optional terminal device specification used when the user is logged on more than once.

Example

```
hello frank
```

Initiates a conversation with the user `frank`.

See also

write

hwconfig

Determines what devices are currently installed. `hwconfig` is primarily used by the system administrator. This information is then used to determine if any conflicts exist, and where new devices can be installed. `hwconfig` effectively reproduces the output generated at boot time.

Syntax

```
hwconfig
```

Messages

hwconfig produces a columnar report with the following
column headings:

Heading	Description
device	What kind of device it is; not the UNIX special device name.
address	The base address for I/O; the range of the driver working space.
vector	The interrupt vector assigned to the device.
dma	The dma channel assigned to the device.
comment	More useful information about the device.

Example

```
hwconfig
```

Produces a list of devices found on the system.

Caution

Third-party device drivers don't always conform to the requirements of this command. In some cases you might not
see the device in the list, or the information displayed is
meaningless.

See also

swconfig

id

id displays your identification to the system. It reports your user name, user id number, group name, and group id number.

Syntax

    id

Example

    id

Shows the id information.

join

Extracts the common lines from two sorted files. One line of output is produced for each line in the two files that match, based on the specified keys.

Syntax

    join [flags] file1 file2

Argument or Option	Description
file1	The first file used in the join; may be a dash (-) to tell join to read from the standard input; thus, join may be a filter in a pipeline.
file2	The second file used in the join.

Flags

Argument or Option	Description
-a*n*	The unmatching lines from either *file1* or *file2* also are produced. *n* may be either a 1 or 2.
-j *n m*	Joins the two files on the *m*th field of file *n*. If *n* is not specified, then the *m*th field of each file is used.
-t *char*	By default, the field separators are tabs, newlines, and spaces. This option causes *char* to be used as the field separator. All instances of *char* are significant. Multiple instances of *char* and the default are treated as one.

Example

```
join to-do-list old-do-list
```

Reports the lines that the two lists have in common.

See also

sort, comm, uniq

kill

Allows you to send a signal to a process that is currently executing. Usually, this command is issued to cause the process to stop executing.

Syntax

```
kill -signal pid
```

Argument or Option	Description
-*signal*	An optional signal that can be sent. The default is 15. 15 stands for SIGTERM. Two other popular signals are 1, which is the equivalent of hanging up the phone as if on a modem, and 9, which is referred to as a sure kill.
pid	The process id of the process you want to send the specified signal. A *pid* is a number used by the system to keep track of the process. The ps command can be used to report the *pid* of a process.

Message

```
kill: permission denied
```

You tried to kill a process that you don't own and/or you are not the super user.

Examples

```
kill 125
```

Sends signal 15 to the process 125. The default signal is 15.

```
kill -1 125
```

Sends signal 1 to the process 125.

```
kill -9 125
```

Sends signal 9. This works if no others do.

Tip

Although -9 is the sure kill, it often is best to try -15 and -1 first. These signals can be caught by the applications and, after they receive them, properly clean up after themselves. Because -9 can't be caught, you may have to do some house cleaning after the process terminates.

Caution

There are instances when even -9 won't kill the process. This is when the process is using a kernel service and can't receive signals. Periodically processes get locked up in this mode. The only way to resolve this is a system shutdown.

See also

sh, ps

l

A link to the command ls. l is just like ls except the default is the long format.

Syntax

l [*flags*] *filelist*

Example

l

Gives a long listing of the current directory.

See also

ls

last

Reads from the /etc/wtmp file and reports the history of
logins and logouts from the system. It can be used to report
who has logged in or what terminals have been used.

Syntax

last -n *limit* -t *tty* *user*

Argument or Option	Description
-n *limit*	Limits the output to *limit* lines.
-t *tty*	Reports the login activity on the terminal device *tty*.
user	Reports the login activity of the user *user*.

Rule

last reads the /etc/wtmp file, which grows until cleared.
On many systems this file is cleared daily. On these systems,
last can only report the information within the last 24-hour
period.

Examples

last frank

Reports the login activity of the user frank.

last

Reports all information, not restricted to a user or terminal.

See also

who, finger, w, ps

lc

Lists directory and file contents in columns sorted alphabetically.

Syntax

```
lc [flags] filelist
```

Example

```
lc
```

Gives a columnar listing of the current directory.

Tip

lf is a link that assumes an invocation of lc -F.

lr assumes lc -R.

lx assumes lc -x.

See also

```
ls
```

line

Reads a line (a string of text up to a newline character) from the standard input and writes it to the standard output. This is useful within a shell script program to read a file and examine its contents or to read a user's input.

Syntax

```
line
```

Examples

```
while INPUT='line'
do
echo "you entered: $INPUT"
done
```

Reads what you type and displays it on-screen.

See also

sh

ln

Creates a link between two files, enabling you to have more than one name to access a file. A directory entry is simply a name to call the file and an i-node number. The i-node number is an index into the file system's table. Therefore, it is easy to have more than one name to i-node reference in the same directory or multiple directories.

A benefit of a link over a copy is that only one copy exists on the disk; therefore, no additional storage is required. Any file may have multiple links.

ln is a link to the cp and mv commands and behaves in a very similar manner. All the rules for these two commands apply here as well, except that ln just makes a link.

ln allows you to link one file to another or to a list of files to use the same name in another directory.

Syntax

```
ln source-file dest-file

ln source-list dest-directory
```

Argument or Option	Description
source-file	The original file.
dest-file	The destination name. This is the name you want the file to go by. It is sort of an alias of the original file.
source-list	A space separated list of the file to link.
dest-directory	The destination directory. This is the directory where you want to have the linked files stored. That is, you want to duplicate the names of the files here just as they were given in the *source-list*.

Example

```
ln letter-to-dad my-letter
```

Enables you to edit either the file letter-to-dad or the file my-letter and modify both of them at the same time.

See also

cp, mv

logname

logname reads the /etc/utmp file to report what name you used to log in to the system.

Syntax

```
logname
```

Example

```
logname
```

Reports the name you used to log in to the system.

lp

Submits a print request to the UNIX system print spooler, or changes the options of a previously entered request. Print requests are spooled, thereby, enabling you to move on to other work.

Syntax

```
lp [flags] filelist
lp -i id [flags]
```

Flags

Argument or Option	Description
-c	Makes a copy of the original file. Without this option set, a link is established between the original file and the working area of the lp spooler.
-ddest	Specifies the destination of the print request. dest may be either an individual printer or a class of printers. A class of printers is a group of printers accessed under one name.
-f formname -d any	Causes the spooler to print the request only when the specified formname is mounted on the printer. With the -d any flag set, the request goes to any printer

(continues)

Argument or Option	Description
	with *formname* mounted. For example, a *formname* may be the company letterhead.
-H *spec-Handling*	Denotes special handling of the request. Valid values for *spec-Handling* are: hold, resume, and immediate.
-m	Sends a mail message to the user, making the request when the request is printed.
-n *number*	Prints *number* copies of the request.
-o *option*	*option* is completely dependent on the interface script chosen by your system administrator when the printer was defined.
-q *priority*	Assigns the request priority of *priority*. The range of *priority* is 0 to 39 with 0 being the highest priority.
-s	Tells lp to be silent. Normally lp responds with the print request-id.
-t *title*	Prints *title* on the banner page.
-w	Writes a message to the user's terminal after the request is printed.

Notes

If the environment variable LPDEST is set, and no -d*dest* is set then the request goes to the *dest* defined by LPDEST; otherwise, the request goes to the system default printer. The lack of a space between -d and *dest* is necessary.

Messages

```
request id is frontdsk-100 (2 files)
```

A successful completion of requesting two files to be sent to the frontdsk printer.

```
lp: destination "frontdk" non-existent
```

A request to print to a printer called frontdk was not granted because the system doesn't know about any printers named frontdk.

```
lp: can't access file "monday_repots"
lp: request not accepted
```

An attempt was made to print a file named monday_repots. However, no file existed by that name. In this case it looks like reports was misspelled.

Examples

```
lp myfile
```

Prints the file myfile to the default printer.

```
lp -dfrontdsk myfile
```

Prints the file myfile to the printer named frontdsk.

```
lp myfile my_other_file
```

Prints the two files myfile and my_other_file.

```
date ¦ lp
```

Sends the date to the default printer. This demonstrates how lp may be used at the end of a pipeline to get a printout of the pipeline's output.

Tip

Use the -s option when defining printers for applications. This way a request-id does not show up on-screen and confuse the user.

See also

lpstat, mail, enable, disable, cancel

lprint

Prints to a local printer attached to your terminal.

Syntax

```
lprint - file
```

Argument or Option	Description
-	Tells lprint to use standard input for the print request, that is, lprint is at the end of a pipeline.
file	Tells lprint to print the file file.

Rules

The - and file options are mutually exclusive. The user must have the proper settings on the terminal to communicate with the printer. lprint uses /etc/termcap entries PN and PS to start and stop the print request, respectively. lprint is a direct printer; it is not a spooled operation. The use of your terminal is forfeited until the request is done or the printer's buffer has absorbed the request.

Message

```
lprint: terminal does not support local printing
```

The terminal type as defined by the TERM environment variable does not have the PN and PS entries defined in the /etc/termcap file.

Example

```
lprint myfile
```

Prints myfile to the printer attached to the user's terminal.

See also

lp, termcap

lpstat

Shows the status of the lp spooler system and print requests.

Syntax

```
lpstat [flags]
```

Flags

Argument or Option	Description
-a *list*	Shows the acceptance status of the printers in *list*.
-c *list*	Shows the class names of the printers in *list*, and their members.
-d	Shows the lp spooler's system default destination.
-f *list* -l	Verifies that the forms listed in *list* are defined to the lp spooler.
-o *list* -l	Shows the status of the print request queued for the printers in *list*. The -l flag gives more detail on the request.

(continues)

Argument or Option	Description
-p *list*	Shows the status of the printers in *list*. Usually used to see if the printer is enabled or if not, why.
-r	Shows if the scheduler is running or not. If the scheduler isn't running, then no print jobs can be scheduled to print. No printing takes place.
-s	Shows a status summary of the spooler. Lists if the scheduler is running, the default printer, and the printer names and the devices associated with them.
-t	Shows all status information. Equivalent to -acdusr.
-u *list*	Shows the status of the printer request similar to that of -o, but for a list of users instead of printers.
-v *list*	Shows a list of printers and the devices associated with them.

Note

Whenever *list* is used, it may be left blank. This causes the flag used to respond with all entries that apply to that flag.

Messages

```
frontdsk-100    sue     245     Sep 15 20:13 on frontdsk
```

This is a sample of the output generated by lpstat with no options, when issued by the user sue after making a print request. The first field, frontdsk-100, is the request-id. The second field, sue, is sue's user name. The third field, 245, is

the size of the request in bytes. The fourth field, Sep 15
20:13, is the date and time that the request was made. And
the last field, on frontdsk, is a status message reporting that
the request is currently being printed.

Examples

    lpstat

Shows the outstanding print requests for the user entering
the command.

    lpstat -u

Shows the outstanding print requests for all users. Notice
how the *list* parameter that caused all users to show was not
supplied.

    lpstat -t

Shows all status information.

    lpstat -s

Shows the system default printer, the devices for each printer
on the system, and whether the scheduler is running.

Tip

When using the -t option and you have more than four
printers, this is a lot of information to see on-screen. You can
pipe it to lp or a pager, such as more, so the information does
not scroll off your screen.

See also

    lp

ls

Lists the files found in the file system.

Syntax

```
ls [flags] filelist
```

Flags

Argument or Option	Description
-A	Shows all files including hidden files. Hidden files start with a period. Does not show current directory (.) or the parent directory (..).
-a	Shows all files including current directory and the parent directory.
-C	Columnar output, sorted down the columns
-x	Columnar output, sorted across the columns
-d	Treats each entry as a directory.
-l	Gives a long listing. A long listing shows details about the files, such as the type of the file, the permissions, the link/directory count, the owner, the group, the size in bytes, when the file was last modified, and the file name. The file types are as follows:

-	Normal file
d	Directory
b	Block special device (disks)
c	Character special device (terminals)

ls -m = comma separated list

Argument or Option	Description
	p Named pipe
	s Semaphore
	m Shared memory
	The permissions are three clusters of three bytes each. Each cluster represents the permissions for the owner, group, and other. The permissions are as follows:
	r Read access
	w Write access
	x Execute access
-t	Sorts by the time last modified. Used with the -l flag.
-u	Sorts by the time last accessed. Used with the -t flag.
-c	Sorts by the time the i-node information last changed. Used with the -t flag.
-r	Reverses the sort order.
-i	Shows the i-node number of the file in the first column.
-F	Places a / after directory entries, and an * after executable programs.

-R = recursive → list subdir contents too
-1 = 1 column output

Message

```
/bin/ls: arg list too long
```

You have asked ls to process an argument list that has more characters in it than can be handled. The maximum number of characters in an argument list is 5,120.

Examples

    ls

Lists the files in the current directory in one long column.

    ls -C

Lists the files in the current directory broken up into columns.

    ls -l

Gives a long listing of the files in the current directory.

    ls -ltr /usr/spool/uucppublic

Gives a long listing, sorted by modification time, in descending order of the files found in the directory /usr/spool/uucppublic.

Tip

Use -d when you want to find the characteristics of a directory. Otherwise the contents of the directory are shown and not the directory itself.

lc is a link to ls that assumes the option of -C.

l is a link to ls that assumes the -l option.

lx is a link to ls that assumes the -x option.

See also

    chmod

mail

Enables you to communicate with other users not only on your local machine—but with the right kinds of connections—to the larger computing community as well. This is the electronic mail facility of UNIX, an extremely handy and powerful tool. mail provides a means of passing messages throughout the office without having to wait for a scheduled mail run. Furthermore, users can catalog incoming mail and use the mail system as a to-do list and filing system to track correspondence.

Syntax

```
mail [flags] usernames
```

Flags

Argument or Option	Description
-e	Tests to see if there is any mail in your incoming mailbox. There is no visible output when this option is used. Useful for the shells if statement or with the shell's && and ¦¦ operators.
-f file	Opens file to read mail from instead of your incoming mailbox. If file is omitted, then the filename mbox is used.
-F	Stores outgoing mail in a file name the same as that of the first recipient of the message. Useful to keep a log of all the mail messages you've sent.
-H	Shows a header summary of the mailbox contents only.
-i	Causes mail to ignore interrupts while constructing mail messages; can be useful when working over noisy dial-up lines.
-n	Causes mail to not initialize from the system mailrc file. The mailrc file sets various options to customize the mail environment

(continues)

Argument or Option	Description
	for each site; a user may have a `mailrc` file also. This is typically called `.mailrc` in the user's home directory.
-N	Causes mail not to print a summary header of the mailboxes' contents.
-s *subject*	Sets the subject line in the mail header to *subject*.
-u *user*	Reads *user*'s incoming mailbox.

Note

The -u *user* flag is only possible if the system administrator has set the permissions on the incoming mailboxes to allow this.

Message

```
No messages.
```

Means that you have invoked the mail utility with no flags set and your incoming mailbox is empty; you have no mail.

Examples

```
mail
```

Invokes the mail utility and enables you to read your mail.

```
mail -u sue
```

Invokes the mail utility to read sue's mailbox.

```
mail sue -s "soccer games(kids)"
```

Invokes the mail utility to send a message to sue on the subject of a soccer games for the kids.

```
mail sue -s "soccer scores" < scores
```

Sends a message to sue with a subject heading of "soccer scores" from a prepared file called scores.

```
date ¦ mail sue -s "date"
```

Demonstrates how mail is used at the end of a pipeline to mail the results of the pipeline to a user. In this case, the date to sue.

```
mail kim john sally
```

Invokes the mail utility to start construction of a message to three people: kim, john, and sally.

Caution

You have to be particularly deliberate when setting up a good structure to catalog your mail files. Otherwise, you might find yourself with mail files throughout the file system. If you want to catalog or save messages, talk to your system administrator about a good approach for this. The administrator may already have the structure in place for you.

Tip

For more information, read the user's guide and tutorial provided with your system.

See also

write

mesg

Enables other users to write to your terminal. This controls whether you allow a user to use the write command to your terminal.

Syntax

```
mesg n y
```

Argument or Option	Description
n	Does not allow users to send messages to your terminal.
y	Allows users to send messages to your terminal.
	No option specified shows the status of your terminal availability to messages.

Note

The default state of your terminal. This command enables users to write to your terminal.

Messages

```
is y
```

Your terminal allows others to write to it.

```
is n
```

Your terminal does not allow others to write to it.

Examples

```
mesg
```

Shows whether users can or can't write to your terminal.

    mesg n

Disallows the writing of messages to your terminal.

    mesg y

Allows users to write to your terminal.

Caution

It is a good idea to set root's .profile file to include the command mesg n. Many terminals have an escape sequence that puts them into echo command mode. That is, what is supplied by the user writing to root's terminal is in effect, executed by root. This is a serious security problem.

See also

    write

mkdir

Creates new directories in the file system.

Syntax

    mkdir -m mode -p dirnames

Argument or Option	Description
-m mode	Sets the directory permissions to mode at the time of creation.
-p	Creates all nonexistent parent directories. See example that follows.

Message

    cannot access letters/

You attempted to create a directory and a parent in the list
didn't exist. In this case, that parent was letters. Use the -p
option.

Examples

    mkdir letters

Creates the directory letters.

    mkdir -p letters/personal letters/work

Makes the directories letters/personal and letters/work. If
the directory letters had not existed, the -p flag would have
caused the directory letters to be created also; otherwise, an
error message would have resulted.

See also

    rm, rmdir, chmod

mknod

Makes special files. *Special files* are considered one of the
following kinds of files: devices, named pipes, semaphores,
and shared memory.

Syntax

    mknod *file_name* [*flags*]

Flags

Argument or Option	Description
b *major minor*	Makes a block special file with major number *major* and minor number *minor*.
c *major minor*	Creates a character special file rather than a block special file.
p	Makes a named pipe.
s	Makes a semaphore.
m	Makes a shared date (memory) file.

Rule

Only the super user can make block and character special files.

Message

```
mknod: must be super user
```

You attempted to make a block or character special file and you don't have super user privileges.

Example

```
mknod my_pipe p
```

Creates a named pipe called my_pipe.

mnt

Enables regular users to mount and unmount file systems similar to those offered to the system administrator through mount and umount. The system administrator can limit access to some or all file systems.

Syntax

```
mnt -tu dirname

umnt dirname
```

Argument or Option	Description
-u	Causes mnt to behave as umnt, and unmounts the file system.
-t	Prints a table of information about the file system.

Rule

The directory you want to mount must be defined by the system administrator in the file /etc/default/filesys with an entry of mount=yes. Otherwise this command fails.

Message

```
Device busy
```

An attempt was made to either mount a device that is in use, or unmount a device that is in use (an open file, the current directory, for example).

Examples

```
mnt /mnt
```

Mounts a device to the default mount directory /mnt.

```
umnt /mnt
```

Unmounts a device that is mounted to the default mount directory /mnt.

See also

```
mount
```

more

more is a general purpose pager. Use more to view text that
scrolls off the screen. more also provides some handy text
search capabilities using regular expressions.

Syntax

```
more [flags] filenames
```

Flags

Argument or Option	Description
-n	n is an integer used to set the window size to n lines long. The window size controls how many lines appear on-screen.
-c	As more pages through the text, it draws each line from top to bottom by clearing the line and then drawing the next line. Normally, more clears the screen and then draws each line.
-d	Displays the prompt Hit space to continue, Rubout to abort in place of the default more prompt.
-f	Counts logical lines rather than screen lines. Long lines wrap around the screen and are normally counted as a new line by more, the -f flag turns off the counting of the wrapped portion of long lines.
-l	Does not treat the ^L (formfeed) character specially. Normally, more treats the ^L the same as the window filling up by pausing.

(continues)

Argument or Option	Description
-r	Shows carriage returns as ^M.
-v	Shows all control characters as ^C, where C is the character used to generate the control character. Those above DEL are shown as M-C, where C is the character without the high bit set.
-s	Multiple blank lines are suppressed and treated as one.
-w	Waits at the end of the file for user-supplied control of quit. Normally, more quits at the end of the file.

Note

For the -c option to work, the terminal must support the clear to end of line capability.

Messages

    filename: No such file or directory

You tried to view a file that doesn't exist.

    filename: not a text file

You tried to view a file that is not a text file. more tries to determine if a file is a text file or not before allowing you to view it. *filename* is substituted with the name you asked for.

    dirname: directory

You tried to use more to view a directory file. *dirname* is substituted with the name you asked for.

Examples

```
more letter-to-dad
```

Displays a text file called letter-to-dad.

```
ls -l /dev ¦ more
```

Demonstrates how more is used at the end of a pipeline to control the output of the pipeline.

Tips

While using the more utility, press h for a list of other possible actions to use.

Set the environment variable MORE to options you want to have set every time you invoke the more utility. For example, if you always want the -v and -w options set, enter the following in your .profile:

```
MORE="-v -w"; export MORE
```

If, while viewing a file, you realize you want to change something, just enter the v command. This boots the vi text editor and allows you to make the changes you want. Exit the editor, and you are returned to the more utility.

If you know that you want to look at a section of the text that contains a certain set of characters, enter the / command followed by a regular expression. This searches for the regular expression you entered. See the ed command in the reference manual supplied with your system for definitions of regular expressions; these are powerful tools.

See also

vi, ed, pg, pr, cat

mv

Renames a file or moves it to a new directory, or both. mv also lets you rename a directory.

Syntax

```
mv -f file1 file2

mv -f dir1 dir2

mv -f filelist dir
```

Argument or Option	Description
-f	Normally mv prompts you if the destination file exists and write permission is turned off. This causes mv to do the move without prompting.
file1	The source file name.
file2	The destination file name (new name).
dir1	The source directory name.
dir2	The destination directory name (new name).
filelist	A space separated list of file names. When this option is used the files retain their names, but are moved to the new directory dir.
dir	The destination directory.

Note

mv cannot physically move a directory; it can only rename it.

Messages

> mv: *filename*: *mode* mode

filename already exists, and the mode of the file doesn't permit it to be overwritten. A response to this prompt with anything starting with a y causes the move to take place; otherwise, the move is ignored. If the -f option is used, the prompt is not shown and the move takes place. *mode* is the mode the file has. Modes are numbers representing permissions.

> mv: *filename* and *filename* are identical

You tried move a file to itself.

> mv: cannot access *filename*

You tried to move a file that doesn't exist.

Examples

> mv letters letter

Changed the file name letters to letter.

> mv letter $HOME/trashcan

Here trashcan is a directory in the user's home directory. This is a useful way to remove files because they are easier to recover if you do not really want to delete them.

Caution

mv doesn't prompt for confirmation of the move unless the destination file already exists and the mode of the file prohibits writing. Because mv first removes the destination file, you may lose a file you do not mean to lose.

Caution

Consider the following directory listing from the `lc` command:

```
customer.dat   inventory.dat
customer.idx   inventory.idx
```

An accidental entry of `mv customer*` where you forgot to supply a destination directory causes the `customer.idx file` to be wiped out. When a wild card expands to only two files and you forget to give the destination directory, you wipe out the second file in the expansion.

Caution

Because `mv` first removes the destination file, if it exists, before doing the move, any links that had been established with the destination file are lost. If you have to maintain those links, you need to first copy the file to the destination name, then remove the original file.

Note

`ln`, `cp`, and `mv` are linked to each other; they determine their actions based on how they are invoked.

See also

rm, cp, ln, copy, chmod

newgrp

Changes your current group id, allowing you to work with that group's files.

Syntax

```
newgrp - group
```

With no options, newgrp returns you to the group you are in when you log in.

Argument or Option	Description
-	If this option is given, the user is logged in under this group id.
group	This is the group id under which you want to become active. *group* must be set up in /etc/group, and the user must be in the list; otherwise, access is denied.

Note

With no options, newgrp returns you to the group you are in when you log in.

Messages

```
unknown group
```

This message means you asked to change to a group id that does not exist.

```
Passwd:
```

You asked to change to a group id for which a password exists. You must enter the correct group password or access to the group is denied.

```
Sorry
```

Access to the group is denied. Either your user name is not in the list of valid users for the group, or you entered an incorrect group password.

Example

```
newgrp admin
```

Changes your group id to admin.

See also

id

news

Reads posted news. Articles are posted to the /usr/news directory. /usr/news is a publicly accessible directory for posting information to share with other users. Articles are simple text files created with any editor. Do not confuse this news facility with USENET news.

Syntax

```
news [flags]
```

Flags

Argument or Option	Description
-a	Shows all news items, regardless of how current they are.
-n	Shows just the names of the articles rather than their contents.
-s	Reports the status of the file; shows if there are any articles to read.
items	Enables you to specify which articles you want to read. Separate each item with a space.

Rule

news places a file named .news_time in your home directory. It uses the time and date of this file to compare to the articles in the /usr/news directory to determine if an article has been read.

Message

    cannot open *item*

You asked to read a specific article and that article does not exist.

Example

    news

Asks that only current articles be printed.

See also

    mail, write

nice

Lowers the scheduling priority level of a process. This utility is appropriately named—you are being nice if you use it.

Syntax

    nice -*increment command*

Argument or Option	Description
increment	The amount by which to change the scheduling priority. Processes are normally given a scheduling priority of 20. *increment* may be any integer in the range 0-39.
command	The command (with its arguments) you want to run with the specified nice factor.

Rule

When using the C shell, this command doesn't apply because the C shell has its own nice command.

Example

Suppose you want to run a large batch job called mass-update. Running the following command lowers the priority from the default value of 20 to 30.

```
nice -10 mass-update
```

Tip

The super user may enter an *increment* as a negative number. –10, for example, increases the scheduling priority of the command.

nl

Adds line numbers to a file. If text files are used by many people, line numbers are a useful reference.

Syntax

```
nl [flags] file
```

Flags

Argument or Option	Description
-b*type*	Specifies how the body of the text is numbered. *type* may be any of the following:
	a All lines.
	t Printable text only (default).
	n No lines (no numbering).
	p*str* Only those lines containing the string *str*.
-h*type*	Same as -b for the header. n is the default type.
-f*type*	Same as -b for the footer. n is the default type.
-p	Does not restart numbering at logical page breaks.
-v*init*	*init* is the number at which to start the logical page numbering (default is 1).
-i*incr*	*incr* is the amount to increment the numbering (default is 1).
-s*char*	*char* is the character used to separate the numbering from the text of the file (default is a tab).
-w*width*	*width* is the amount of space the numbering can have (default is 6).

Rules

file can be left blank. If *file* is left blank, then the standard input is assumed; this allows nl to be the filter program in a pipeline.

nl's output is always to the standard output.

nl can distinguish header, body, and footer sections only if lines containing nothing but the following are used to denote the beginning of that section:

Section	Indicated by
Header	\:\:\:
Body	\:\:
Footer	\:

Message

```
INVALID OPTION (-C) - PROCESSING TERMINATED
```

You gave nl an option *C*; *C* is not a valid option. *C* becomes the option you tried to use.

Example

```
nl first-draft ¦ lp
```

Numbers all lines in the file called first-draft, and sends the output to the default printer.

See also

pr

od

od stands for octal dump. od shows the octal representations of a file's contents. Viewers such as pg and more are designed for text-based files. Text-based files consist of printable characters. Binary files are typically files generated by a database, but today, most spreadsheets and word-processing documents are also binary. At times, you need to look at an area of a binary file, and more doesn't work.

Syntax

od [-bcdox] [*file*] [*offset_spec*]

Argument or Option	Description
file	The name of the file to process. If left blank, then the standard input is used.
offset_spec	An offset specifier that determines when the output starts. *offset_spec* by default is the number of bytes to skip (expressed as an octal number). You can provide either one or both of the following modifiers.
	. The number given is interpreted as a decimal number, not octal.
	b The number, whether octal or decimal, is not bytes, but blocks (512 bytes).
	If no *file* is given, then *offset_spec* must be preceded by a plus sign (+) as in this example: +10.b -·. This example specifies that 10 (decimal) blocks are skipped from the standard input.

Flags

Argument or Option	Description
b	Shows the octal number of each byte (8 bits).
c	Shows printable characters as themselves, non-printable as octal numbers, and the following special characters:

	\b	Backspace
	\0	Null
	\f	Formfeed
	\n	Newline
	\r	Carriage return
	\t	Tab

Argument or Option	Description
d	Shows decimal words (16 bits)
o	Shows octal words (16 bits)
x	Shows hexadecimal words (16 bits)

Message

    od: cannot open ben.1

You tried to open a file (ben.1) that od cannot find.

Examples

Suppose you are working with an application, and when you press F1 to bring up a help screen, nothing happens. You can double-check the software configuration to ensure that F1 is the correct key. Each key on a keyboard returns a set of characters. You can validate the output of the F1 key against the documentation for this terminal type to see if someone reprogrammed the key.

```
od -c
```

Reads from standard input anything you type until you press a newline (the Enter key) followed by Ctrl-d. It then displays those keystrokes on-screen using printable characters when it can and octal for all others. You press the F1 key, the Enter key, and, finally, Ctrl-d to see what sequence returns.

See also

hd, more, pg

pack

Compresses or packs files so that their storage requirements are less. This is most useful when sending files across a mode because a smaller file takes less time to transfer. pcat works like cat but on packed files.

Syntax

```
pack - filenames
```

Argument or Option	Description
-	If the - is specified, more statistical information is shown about the packing of the files.
filenames	A space delimited list of the files to be packed.

Notes

pack obtains about a 40 percent reduction on text files, and only about 15 percent on binary files. (This is just a rough estimate; actual compression rates vary for each file.)

Files that are packed are renamed with a .z extension added.

Messages

```
pack: filename: xx.xx% Compression
```

filename was able to obtain a compression percent of *xx.xx*.

```
pack: filename: cannot open
```

filename does not exist, or you don't have permission to access it.

```
pack: filename: already packed
```

filename looks as though it is already in a packed format.

```
pack: filename: cannot pack a directory
```

filename is a directory; you can't pack directories.

```
pack: filename: file name too long
```

If working on a UNIX system that still limits file names to 14 characters, you can get this message. *filename* must have more than 12 characters; therefore, there isn't enough room to append the .z.

```
pack: filename: has links
```

The file you wanted to pack has links; you cannot pack a file with links.

```
pack: filename.z: already exists
```

There is a file name with the .z extension already; pack won't overwrite it.

```
pack: filename: no savings - file not changed
```

Running pack on the file does not result in any savings; nothing is done to the file.

```
pcat: filename: cannot open
```

filename doesn't exist, or you don't have permissions to access it.

```
pcat: filename.z: not in packed format
```

A file with the .z extension exists; the file isn't in a packed format.

Examples

```
pack old-letters/*
```

Packs all the files in the directory old-letters.

```
pcat old-letters/letter-to-dad ¦ more
```

Looks at the file letter-to-dad.z, unpacks it, and pipes the output through the utility more.

See also

compress, uncompress, zcat, cat, unpack

passwd

Maintains user passwords. Also, system administrators can use this command to administer the user directory. It is strongly recommended that you use the system administrator's shell provided with your system to administer user directories as they are typically menu driven and allow you to back out of actually implementing the change.

Syntax

```
passwd
```

The passwd command actually has many options not shown here. These other options are relevant only if you are a system administrator, so they are not discussed here. All features on password management are clearly defined in the system administrator's guide provided with your system.

The following are two of the password management features:

- *Locks.* An account may have a lock on it. This prevents the account from being used. Locks can be applied automatically if there are more than a system-defined number of tries to log in under that user name.

- *Expiration.* A password can expire after a certain amount of time has passed. This is sometimes referred to as *password aging.* You also may require a user to change his or her password the next time he or she logs in. You can limit how soon a user may change their password again, thus discouraging changing the password back to the old password.

Notes

You have to be an administrator to change someone else's password.

Passwords should be chosen so that they are easy to remember but hard to guess. This almost seems like a contradiction in terms. However, good password selection is crucial to a secure system.

Messages

```
Permission denied
```

You attempted to change the password for a user that doesn't exist, or you are not a system administrator or super user and attempted to change a password other than your own.

```
Sorry
```

passwd prompts you for your old password when trying to enter a new one. You entered your old password incorrectly. You have to invoke passwd again to change your password.

Example

```
passwd
```

Places you into the password change program. You are first prompted for your old password. Depending on your system's configuration, you may be allowed to choose a password for yourself, it may generate one for you, or you may be able to choose which to do.

paste

Produces columnar output from one or more files, where each file contributes a column of the output. paste often is used with cut to reorder columns in a file.

Syntax

```
paste -ddelim filelist

paste -s -ddelim filelist
```

Argument or Option	Description
-ddelim	Specifies what character is used to delimit each column (tab is the default).
filelist	A list of files to paste together. Can be - to signify standard input.
-s	Causes paste to traverse each file separately. This uses lines in the file for each column. The first line is the first column, the second line the second column, and so on.

Note

The output of paste is always standard output.

Messages

```
line too long
```

The output of paste using the files supplied exceeds 511 characters on a line.

```
too many files
```

You tried to paste together more than 12 files. You have to do it in two or more passes to complete the job.

Examples

```
ls -l ¦ tee /tmp/tmp.$$ ¦ cut -f5 -d' ' >/tmp/sz.$$
cut -f9 -d' ' /tmp/tmp.$$ ¦ paste - /tmp/sz.$$
rm /tmp/*.$$
```

At first this might look like a lot to swallow, but look at it piece by piece. This command takes the output of l and produces a listing with the name of the file followed by its size in bytes. The result of l is piped through tee to allow you to store a copy of the l's output for later use (/tmp /tmp.$$). The pipe flows through tee to the first cut command that extracts the field holding the size and stores the field in a file for later use (/tmp/sz.$$). The second cut extracts the name field, piping this to paste. paste accepts standard input as its first column and the file /tmp/sz.$$ as the second column. Lastly, clean up by removing the temporary files.

See also

cut, rm, tee, pr, grep

pcat

See pack.

pcpio

pcpio stands for portable copy in out (cpio). It reads and writes the format of the cpio Archive/Interchange File Format specified in IEEE Std. 1003.1-1988. pcpio behaves very much like cpio, but it is an archiver. pcpio is useful not only for making backups, but also for moving files in the file system.

Syntax

```
pcpio -o [flags]

pcpio -i [flags] filelist

pcpio -p [flags] dirname
```

Argument or Option	Description
-o	Creates the archive, that is, generates the output.
-i	Copies from a previously created archive.
-p	Accepts a list of files from the standard input and passes them to the specified directory. Useful for copying whole directory structures on the file system.
filelist	A space separated list of files to extract from the archive. May contain wild cards. The wild cards supported are the same as the simple regular expression expansion provided by the shell (sh).

	!	Means not
	?	Matches a single character
	*	Matches any number of characters
	[]	Matches the set of characters specified between the brackets

If you use a wild card, enclose *filelist* in quotation marks ("). Otherwise, the shell expands them. A weakness of another archiver, tar, is that it doesn't support wild cards; it relies on the shell to expand its list of files.

dirname	The destination directory for the files given pcpio with the -p option.

Flags

Argument or Option	Description
-B	Signifies a blocking factor of 5,120 bytes per record. Used with the -o and -i options and only when sending the output to, or reading the input from, a character special device.
-a	Resets the access times of files after the copy is completed. If used with -l, files with links are not affected. Used with -o or -i.
-c	Creates or reads the header information in an archive in an ASCII character format. This creates headers readable on other platforms. For example, you can move an archive created on an X86 Intel-based machine to a 68X Motorola-based machine. Used with -o or -i.
-d	Creates the directories as needed. If the directories don't exist, pcpio creates them. Used with -p or -i.
-f	Changes the interpretation of *filelist*. Normally *filelist* is a list of files to extract. When you use the -f option, *filelist* is the list of files not to extract. Used with -i.
-l	Links files rather than copying them, if possible. Used with -p.
-m	Retains the modification times of files as found in the archive. Normally the modification times change to the current time. This does not affect directories. Used with -i and -p.

Argument or Option	Description
-r	To rename the files in *filelist*. You are prompted for each file in *filelist* for the new name, if none is given, the file is skipped. Used with -o or -i.
-t	Prints a list of files in the archive. Used with -i.
-u	Extracts files from an archive unconditionally. Normally pcpio extracts a file from the archive only if the file is newer than the file on the file system. Used with -p or -i.
-v	Signifies verbose mode. Tells pcpio to give a status report. Used with -i.

Messages

```
pcpio -o[BacLv]
pcpio -i[Bcdmrtuvf] {pattern...}
pcpio -p[adlLmruv] directory
```

The message you most likely see is a usage clause showing you the necessary syntax to use pcpio. If such a message appears, you probably forgot to provide an option; check your command line again.

Examples

```
ls | pcpio -oBc >/dev/rfd096ds15
```

Lists the current directory passing the list through the pipeline to pcpio. pcpio uses the input from the pipeline as its list of files to copy. It copies this list of files to the standard output with a blocking factor of 5120; the header information is written in a portable ASCII format. This output is redirected to the character special device /dev/rfd096ds15 (a high-density 5 1/4-inch floppy disk).

```
pcpio -iBcdm "*.ltr" </dev/rfd096ds15
```

Extracts the files ending in `.ltr` from the floppy disk, and places them in the current directory. Any subdirectories are created as needed. The file's modification times are the same as at the time the archive was created.

```
ls ¦ pcpio -pdl /usr/newdir
```

Copies the list generated by `ls` to the directory `/usr/newdir`, creates any directories needed, and links rather than copies when possible.

Tip

`pcpio` with the `-i` and `-o` options is a *filter program*; it accepts input from the standard input and directs its output to the standard output. `pcpio` can be anywhere in pipeline, as long as the input to the `-o` option is a list of file names, and the input to the `-i` option is the result of a previous `-o`. The `-p` option is not a true filter, because the output is a specified directory.

See also

copy, tar, cpio, ptar, find

Prompt Commands

Some of `pg`'s commands may be preceded by an optional *address*. An *address* is interpreted as either pages or lines based on whether the command is a line-oriented command or a page-oriented command. An *address* preceded by either a plus (+) or a minus (-) causes `pg` to go forward or backward relative to the current line/page. In other words, + means forward *address* lines/pages, and - means backward *address* lines/pages. An unsigned *address* is absolute with respect to the beginning of the file (for example, 100 for a line-oriented command is the 100th line, and 100 for a page-oriented command is the 100th page).

Command	Description
address <return key>	If you press the return key, pg moves *address* pages. The default *address* is +1.
address l	Causes pg to move to *address* line. A signed *address* scrolls forward or backward the number of lines specified. An unsigned *address* displays a full screen starting at the specified *address*. The default *address* is +1
address d or <CTRL> d	Moves in half screens. The default *address* is +1.
. or <CTRL>l	Redraws the screen.
$	Moves to the end of the current input file. When used in a pipe line this command may not behave as expected.
i/search_expr/	Search forward to match the regular expression *search_expr*, and look for the *i*[th] occurrence of this expression. *i*'s default is 1. Searches to the end of the file.
i^search_expr^ *i*?search_expr?	Same as *i*/search but searches backward to the beginning of the file. Either form is valid.

Note

Each of the preceding search commands can have a trailing modifier to affect where the found text is displayed. Normally pg displays the found text at the top of the screen. The modifier specified resets the default behavior for all searches. The modifiers in the following table are valid.

Modifier	Description
b	Displays the found text on the bottom.
m	Displays the found text in the middle.
t	Resets the displays to the top.

If no modifier is used, *search_expr* doesn't require a trailing /, ^, or ?. When using the modifiers, the trailing characters must be included so that the modifiers are not confused with the *search-_expr*.

Argument or Option	Description
i n	Skip the current file; start displaying the ith file in *file_list*. The default for *i* is 1.
i p	Same as n but for the previous file.
i w	Displays another window (screen full). Or if *i* is given, it resets the window size.
s *file_name*	Save the current file to the file name specified by *file_name*.
h	Gives a help message on available commands.
q or Q	Quits pg.
!*command*	Runs your current shell as defined by the environment variable SHELL and passes *command* to it for processing.

Messages

```
ben: No such file or directory
```

You tried to give pg a file that doesn't exist; in this case that file name is ben.

```
Pattern not found:
```

While at the command line (the prompt) of pg, you entered a search string and that string is not found in the file.

Examples

```
pg letter-to-dad
```

Looks at a text file called letter-to-dad.

```
ls -l /dev ¦ pg
```

Demonstrates how you can use more at the end of a pipeline to control the pipeline's output.

See also

vi, ed, more, pr, cat

pg

A general purpose pager. Similar to more, pg enables you to view text files. pg enables you to go backward through a file, and more does not. However, more enables you to edit the contents you are viewing by invoking the vi editor; pg doesn't.

Syntax

```
pg [flags] filelist
```

Argument or Option	Description
`filelist`	A list of space delimited file names; if left blank pg reads from the standard input.

Flags

Argument or Option	Description
-	Specifies that standard input is used to read the text from.
`-number`	Sets the window size to `number`. The amount of lines shown at a time is `number` (default is 1 less than the `li` parameter in `/etc/termcap`).
`-p message`	Uses `message` as the prompt at the end of each window's display. An optional %d may be used in `message` to show the current page number. Enclose `message` in quotation marks (") to ensure that the shell does no wild-card expansion. The default prompt is `:`.
`-e`	pg won't pause at the end of each file.
`-n`	Causes pg to behave like more and recognize the end of the command as soon as a letter is pressed. Normally, each command must be followed by a carriage return.
`-s`	All messages and prompts use "standout mode." Standout mode is usually reverse video.
`+number`	Starts showing text only after `number` of lines is encountered.

Argument or Option	Description
+/*pattern*/	Starts showing text when *pattern* is found. *pattern* uses the rules of regular expressions. See the ed command in your user's reference for a definition of regular expressions.

Note

If the terminal type defined by the environment variable TERM can't be found in /etc/termcap, then the terminal type of dumb is used.

Messages

```
pg: dirname is a directory
```

You tried to invoke pg to read a file that was a directory. *dirname* is substituted by the name you gave it.

```
pg: No such file or directory
```

You tried to view a file that doesn't exist, or you don't have permission to read the file.

Examples

```
pg letter-to-dad
```

Displays a text file called letter-to-dad.

```
ls -l /dev ¦ pg
```

Demonstrates how pg may be used at the end of a pipeline to control the output of the pipeline.

Tip

While using the pg utility, press the h command for a list of other possible actions to use.

Tip

Pressing / while in pg places you in search mode. ^(caret) or ?
places you in reverse search mode. Search mode uses regular
expressions as described previously for *pattern*.

Tip

Commands preceded by a negative number cause pg to do
the action of the command backward the number entered.
For example, if the command is preceded by –10, the command performs the action after it goes back 10 pages; it does
not perform the action on each page as it goes back.

Tip

Some UNIX applications use a pager. Many of these applications look for an environment variable called PAGER. Setting
PAGER to the pager you want causes these applications to
give you a more consistent feel when viewing the output.

See also

more, ed, cat, grep

pr

Allows you to do some formatting to a file while printing it
to the standard output. pr also has some of the functionality
of paste and nl built into it.

Syntax

pr [*flags*] *filelist*

Argument or Option	Description
filelist	A space delimited list of files. If left blank, the standard input is read. - can be used as a file name to tell pr to read from the standard input. You can combine file names and the -. This causes pr to read both from the standard input and from the listed files.

Flags

Argument or Option	Description
+page	Begins printing with page *page*. The default is page 1.
-col	Specifies *col* columns of output. This flag assumes the flags -e and -i. The default is 1 column.
-m	Merges the files, printing each file in a column, overriding the -col flag.
-d	Double spaces the output.
-eccol	When reading the input, tabs are replaced with character *c* and expanded to positions (*col* + 1), ((2 * *col*) + 1), ((3 * *col*) + 1), and so on. *c* may be any nondigit character. *col* defaults to every eight positions.
-iccol	Works like -e except on the output of pr, replacing whitespace with the character *c*. Whitespace is spaces, tabs, and so on.

(continues)

Argument or Option	Description
-nc*width*	Selects line numbering. *c* is the character to place between the line number and the normal output (the default is a tab). *width* is how many character positions the number +1 occupies (the default is 5).
-w*length*	Sets the length of the line to *length* lines. For columnar output the default is 72; no limit is assumed otherwise.
-o*offset*	Offsets each line of output by *offset* character positions. (default is 0).
-l*lines*	Sets the length of the page to *lines* lines (default is 66).
-h *string*	Uses *string* as the header instead of the file name.
-p	Causes pr to page the output, pausing at the end of each page (only if the output is associated with a terminal).
-f	Uses a formfeed character between pages. Normally, pr fills the remaining lines with newline characters to cause a page break.
-t	Doesn't print the header or the footer. Normally, pr prints a five line header and footer.
-s*char*	Separates multicolumn output with *char*. Tab is the default.

Messages

    pr: can't open *filename*

pr can't access *filename*. Either it doesn't exist, or you don't have permission to read it.

```
pr: bad option
```

You specified an option pr doesn't understand.

Examples

```
pr -n program.c ¦ lp
```

Formats the file program.c with line numbers and sends the output to the printer.

```
ls ¦ pr -8 -i\ 6 -w132 -l51 ¦ lp
```

Takes the output of the ls command and produces an eight column report separated by a space every six character positions and prints it to a printer that has 8 1/2 × 11-inch paper in it (132 columns by 51 lines).

```
ls /dev ¦ grep "^tty" ¦ fgrep -vx "tty" ¦ \
pr -m - /etc/ttytype ¦ lp
```

Takes the listing of the /dev directory and pipes it through two grep commands, then pipes that result to pr. The first grep extracts all the lines starting with the characters tty. The second grep extracts all the lines that don't exactly match tty (do this to strip out the /dev/tty entry), then merges this with the /etc/ttytype file, sending the results to the printer. This is useful to compare the actual tty devices with entries in the /etc/ttytype file.

See also

cat, grep, fgrep, lp, paste, more, pg

ps

Reports the status of processes. Because processes rapidly progress in their execution path, this report is only a snapshot view of what was happening when you asked. A subsequent invocation of ps may give quite different results.

Syntax

```
ps [flags]
```

Flags

No options shows you a picture of the currently executing processes on your terminal. The following columns are reported:

Column	Description
PID	The process id number used by the kernel to keep track of the process.
TTY	The terminal with which the process is associated.
TIME	The accumulated time spent running the process (CPU time not wall-clock time).
CMD	The name of the process running.
-e	Shows status of every process.
-d	Shows the status all processes, except group leaders.
-f	Gives a full listing. A full listing gives you the user name that invoked the process, and also shows you the original command line used to invoke the process. If ps can't get the command line information it places the name of the process in square brackets [ ]. The following also are shown:

	PPID	The process id of the process that invoked this process (the parent process).
	C	Used for scheduling purposes.
	STIME	The time when the process started.

Column	Description
-l	Gives you a long listing. This gives you a snapshot of the following:

	F	The status flag of the process (01=in core, 10=being swapped).
	S	The state of the process (S=sleeping, R=running, Z=terminated, B=waiting).
	PRI	The current priority of a process. The lower the number, the higher the priority. If a process's priority is less than around 24, usually means the process is in the kernel, and signals can't be caught. Thus, a kill has no effect until its priority is lowered (unkillable process).
	NI	The nice factor used in scheduling.
	ADDR1 ADDR2	The address in memory or disk of the process.
	SZ	The size of the process's user area. This does not include the size of the text portion.
	WCHAN	The kernel event for which the process is waiting.

(continues)

Column	Description
-t*ttys*	Reports the status of the process associated with the terminals listed in *ttys*. *ttys* may be comma delimited or space delimited and enclosed in quotation marks. (You do not need the tty portion of the tty name.)
-p*pids*	Reports the status of the processes with pid numbers of *pids*. *pids* uses the same format as *ttys*.
-u*users*	Reports the status of the processes invoked by the users in the list *users*. *users* uses the same format as *ttys*.
-g*glist*	Reports the status of the processes whose group leaders are in the list *glist*. *glist* uses the same format as *ttys*.

Message

```
ps: illegal option
```

You gave ps a flag that it doesn't understand.

Examples

```
ps
```

Shows you the processes running on your terminal.

```
ps -t01,02
```

Shows the processes running the terminals tty01 and tty02.

```
ps -usue
```

Shows you what process sue is running.

```
ps -elf ¦ more
```

Shows you everything ps can show you. Pipe the output
through more, so that it doesn't race across your screen.

Tip

The -t and -u options are particularly useful for system administrators who have to kill processes for users that have
gone astray.

See also

kill, nice, more, w, who, whodo

ptar

Purpose

Creates portable tar output to conform with the Archive/
Interchange File Format specifications in IEEE Std. 1003.1-
1988. ptar, the *p*ortable *t*ape *ar*chiver creates archives of the
file system.

Syntax

ptar -action[flags] flag-args filelist

Argument or Option	Description
-action	Specifies what action to take on the archive. action can be one of the following:
	c Creates a new archive, or overwrites an existing one.
	r Writes the files named in filelist to the end of the archive.

(continues)

Argument or Option	Description
	t Gives a table of contents of the archive.
	u Updates the archive. Adds the files named in *filelist* to the end of the archive if they aren't found in the archive or if they have been modified since the last write (may take quite a bit of time).
	x Extracts the files named in *filelist*
filelist	The list of files to manipulate, may contain wild cards (see warning below). If *filelist* is a directory, that directory is recursively traversed and matches all files within that directory's substructure.
flag-args	When a flag requires an argument, the arguments are delayed until after all flags are specified. The arguments are listed on the command line in the same order as the flags.

Flags

Argument or Option	Description
-b	Specifies the blocking factor. May be any integer between 1 and 20. The default is 1. You should use this only with raw tape/floppy devices. Requires an argument.

Argument or Option	Description
-f	Specifies the file name to use as the archive. Can be a regular file or a special character device (/dev/ rfd096ds15 for a high-density floppy). If - is used, standard input is read from or written to, depending on the action specified. (You cannot pipe a *filelist* to ptar as with cpio, or pcpio.) Requires an argument.
-l	Tells ptar to display a warning if it can't resolve all links to a file. Normally, ptar is silent about archiving a set of files when not all links are specified. Used only with -c, -r, and -u actions.
-m	Tells ptar to set the modification time to that of the time of extraction. Normally, ptar sets the modification time to that stored on the archive. Not valid with the -t action.
-o	Sets the user and group ids to that of the user extracting from the archive, as opposed to that stored on the archive. Used only with the -x action.
-v	Places ptar into verbose mode. That is, the file names appear on the terminal as ptar processes them. When used with the -t option, ptar gives you a listing similar to the long listing of the ls command.
-w	Causes ptar to wait for you to respond with a y or an n before taking action on the file. Any response starting with the letter y means yes, and any other response means no. Not valid with the -t action.

Rules

When listing the file names, you must be careful to use absolute or relative path names. Files are extracted from the archive in the same way they were created. Furthermore, if you request only a single file to be extracted, you must specify that file name on the command line the same way it was created. For example, suppose you created an archive using the following:

```
ptar -cvf /dev/rfd096ds15 /usr/frank
```

This created an archive of all files in the directory hierarchy /usr/frank. If you want to get back a file called letters-to-mom, you must enter the following:

```
ptar -xf /dev/rfd096ds15 /usr/frank/letters-to-mom
```

If you had specified letters-to-mom in the *filelist*, ptar could not have found the file.

Messages

```
ptar: tape write error
```

Means one of two things: you don't have a floppy disk or tape in the drive; or you have filled up the floppy disk or tape.

```
ptar: tape read error
```

Means you don't have a floppy/tape in the drive.

```
ptar: directory checksum error
```

Means one of two things: you specified the wrong media type for the floppy disk or tape drive; or the tape needs to be rewound. Specifying the wrong media type is a common error. Users have been known to place a 360K floppy disk in the drive and attempt to access it with the /dev/rfd096ds15 device.

Examples

```
ptar -cvf /dev/rfd096ds15 .
```

Creates an archive on the high-density floppy drive of the current directory showing all file names it encounters.

```
ptar -xvf /dev/rfd096ds15
```

Extracts all files found on the floppy and shows the file names it encounters.

```
ptar -cvbf 20 /dev/rfd096ds15 /usr/frank
```

Demonstrates the syntax involved when combining flags that require arguments. It creates an archive of frank's home directory using a blocking factor of 20 and places the archive on the high-density floppy.

```
ptar -cf - /usr/frank ¦ wc -c
```

The value of this particular command is questionable. However, it shows how to use the - to send the output to standard output. It creates an archive of frank's home directory and pipes the output through wc to get a count of the characters. You can use this command to find out how big the archive is.

Caution

Special devices are not placed on the archive.

Caution

You can use wild cards in *filelist*. However, the ptar command doesn't do any wild-card expansion. The shell does the expansion and passes the result to ptar. This can be a problem for novice users who have deleted files and then want to extract them from the archive. Because the file doesn't exist on the file system, the shell can't expand the wild cards to match the nonexistent files. To illustrate, suppose you have a

series of files that all end with the letters .ltr. You can
create an archive of the whole directory using the following
command:

```
ptar -cf /dev/rfd096ds15 .
```

After realizing that you messed up all files ending with .ltr,
you can extract them from the archive:

```
ptar -xf /dev/rfd096ds15 *.lst
```

This restores the fouled .ltr files. However, if the files are
deleted, then ptar doesn't find any files to extract. It cannot
find any more than the following ls command does.

```
ls *.ltr
```

If the files are deleted, you have to specify each one in full
without the use of wild cards. Alternatively, you can use a
prepass with the -t option redirected to a file.

```
ptar -tf /dev/rfd096ds15 >list.tmp
```

Use the following to retrieve all files ending in .lst:

```
ptar -xf /dev/rfd096ds15 'grep ".lst$" list.tmp'
```

See also

tar, cpio, pcpio, backup, restore, xbackup, xrestore, ls,
wc, grep

purge

Purges files by overwriting them. Because removing files with
the rm command doesn't actually change the magnetic image
on the disks and tapes, it is still possible to get to the data.
This command can be useful when dealing with sensitive
data, especially on portable media such as floppy disks and
tapes.

Syntax

```
purge [flags] filelist
```

Argument or Option	Description
filelist	A space delimited list of files to purge. These can be regular files, directories, or special character files.

Flags

Argument or Option	Description
-f	Causes purge to not complain about files that do not exist or on which you do not have sufficient permissions. (A floppy disk or tape not in its drive still generates an error message.)
-r	Recursively traverses any directories specified, and purges all files encountered.
-v	Verbose mode.
-mint	Causes multiple passes. int specifies the number of passes (any integer). The first pass always writes binary zeros. Subsequent passes alternate between binary ones and zeros.

Example

```
purge /dev/rfd096ds15
```

Writes binary zeros to the high-density floppy drive.

pwd

Reports your present working or current directory.

Syntax

```
pwd
```

Messages

```
Cannot open ..

Read error in ..
```

The two previous messages indicate a problem with the file system. Contact a system administrator.

Example

```
pwd
```

Shows the current directory in which you are working.

See also

```
cd
```

rm

Removes files and entire directory structures from the file system.

Syntax

```
rm [flags] filelist
```

Argument or Option	Description
filelist	A space-delimited list of files you want to delete. It may contain directory names as well.

Flags

Argument or Option	Description
-r	Deletes the directories specified in *filelist*. Directories are not deleted unless this flag is used. -r can only delete as many as 17 levels of subdirectories.
-i	Specifies interactive mode. You are prompted for confirmation before the removal takes place. Any response beginning with a Y indicates yes; all others indicate no.
-f	Specifies forced mode. Normally, rm prompts you if you don't have permissions to delete the file. This flag forces the remove without your involvement.
--	Indicates the end of all options. Useful if you have to delete a file name that is the same as one of the options. For example, suppose a file named -f was created by accident, and you want to delete it. The command, rm -f does not accomplish anything because the -f is interpreted as a flag and not the file name. The command rm -- -f, however, successfully removes the file.

Messages

```
rm: filename nonexistent
```

You tried to remove a file that doesn't exist. *filename* is substituted with the file name you supplied.

```
rm: illegal option -- ?
```

You supplied rm with an option it didn't understand. It may be that you are trying to delete a file that starts with a -. See the -- flag.

Examples

```
rm letter-to-dad
```

Deletes the file named letter-to-dad.

```
rm -r oldletters
```

In this example, oldletters is a directory. This deletes all the files in this directory substructure.

```
rm -i sue*
```

Prompts you each time it encounters a file starting with the letters sue to see if the file should be deleted.

See also

rmdir, mv, cp, ln, copy, purge

rmdir

Removes directories.

Syntax

```
rmdir -p -s dirlist
```

Argument or Option	Description
-p	Causes rmdir to delete any parent directories that also become empty after deleting the directories specified in *dirlist*. A status message as to what is, and what is not deleted, is displayed.
-s	Suppresses the messages when the -p option is active.
dirlist	A space-delimited list of directory names. Directories must be empty to be deleted.

Notes

If the sticky bit is set on a directory, the directory is only deleted if at least one of the following is true:

- The parent directory is owned by the user.

- The user owns the directory in *dirlist*.

- The user has write permissions to the directory in *dirlist*.

- The user is the super user (root).

Messages

rmdir: *dirname* non-existent

The directory you tried to remove doesn't exist.

rmdir: *dirname* not a directory

You used rmdir on a file name that isn't a directory.

rmdir: *dirname* not empty

You tried to delete a directory that still contains some files.

Example

```
rmdir letters.1970
```

Deletes a directory that used to hold some old letters.

See also

```
rm
```

sdiff

Runs diff with the files compared side by side. This command can be extremely useful when comparing two versions of a file because the output is easier to read than that of regular diff.

Syntax

```
sdiff [flags] file1 file2
```

Argument or Option	Description
file1	The file in the left column of the output.
file2	The file in the right column of the output.

Flags

Argument or Option	Description
-wwidth	Specifies the output line is to be width characters. The default is 130.
-l	When lines are identical, they appear on the left side only.

Argument or Option	Description
-s	Suppresses the lines that are identical.
-o*filename*	Enables you to merge the two files into a third file specified by *filename*. sdiff prompts with a % after displaying the set of differences. Identical lines are automatically copied to *filename*. Valid responses to the % prompt include:

	l	Use the left column to append to *filename*.
	r	Use the right column to append to *filename*.
	s	Silent mode, doesn't print identical lines.
	v	Turn off silent mode.
	e l	Invokes ed with the left column.
	e r	Invokes ed with the right column.
	e b	Invokes ed with both columns.
	e	Invokes ed with neither column.
	q	Exits sdiff.

Changes made in the editor are transferred to *filename*.

Rule

The output has three columns. The left column is *file1*, the right column is *file2*, and the middle column is one of the following:

Symbol	Meaning
	No symbol, space, means the lines are identical.
<	These lines are found only in *file1*.
>	These lines are found only in *file2*.
¦	These lines are different.

Messages

    sdiff: cannot open: *filename*

You supplied sdiff with a file name, *filename*, that doesn't exist.

    sdiff: Illegal argument: *arg*

You supplied sdiff with an argument, *arg*, that it doesn't understand.

Example

    sdiff letter-to-mom letter.bak

Compares the two files: letter-to-mom and letter.bak.

See also

    diff, diff3, ed

setcolor

Sets various color attributes on the system console. This allows applications written without any color support to appear as if they have color support. It also enables you to set the characteristics of the bell and the cursor.

Syntax

```
setcolor [flags] color1 color2

setcolor -p pitch duration

setcolor -c first last
```

Argument or Option	Description
color1	The first color argument.
color2	A second color argument for the flags that accept it.
-p	Defines how the bell character (^G) acts.
pitch	Sets the pitch (microseconds).
duration	Sets the duration of the bell (fifths of a second).
first	The first scan line of the cursor.
last	The last scan line of the cursor.

Flags

The absence of a flag accepts color1 as the foreground color, and an optional color2 as the background color.

Argument or Option	Description
-n	Sets the screen to "normal." This takes no color arguments, and sets the screen back to a white foreground and a black background.
-b	Sets the screen's background color to color1.

(continues)

Argument or Option	Description
-r	Sets the screen's reverse video foreground color to *color1* and the background reverse video color as *color2*.
-g	Same as -r, except for the graphics characters.
-o	Sets the border to *color1*.

Rules

color1 and *color2* can be any of the following:

blue	magenta	brown	black
lt_blue	lt_magenta	yellow	gray
cyan	white	green	red
lt_cyan	hi_white	lt_green	lt_red

setcolor works only on consoles that support color. The effect of invoking this utility on any other terminal is undefined. Serious damage isn't a real threat, but some really messed up terminal settings can result.

Messages

    setcolor: Invalid color name

You supplied setcolor with a color that is not listed in the table, or you didn't supply a color when one was required.

    setcolor: Unrecognized option

You supplied setcolor with a flag that is not in the list.

Examples

```
setcolor brown black
```

Sets the console's foreground color to brown and its background color to black; makes the console look very much like an amber terminal.

```
setcolor -r red white
```

Sets the reverse foreground to red and the characters to white.

Tip

Invoking setcolor with no options at all gives a usage clause and displays the color table.

Tip

The output of setcolor can be redirected to a tty device. In this way colors are set inside shell scripts for different applications.

Tip

If you type the following at the console all possible combinations of foreground and background color appear.

```
for i in blue lt_blue cyan lt_cyan magenta lt_magenta \
        white hi_white brown yellow green lt_green \
        black gray red lt_red
do
    for j in blue lt_blue cyan lt_cyan magenta \
            lt_magenta white hi_white brown yellow \
            green lt_green black gray red lt_red
    do
    if [ $i = $j ]
        then
        continue
    fi
    setcolor $i $j
```

```
        echo "This is $i foreground and $j background"
        echo "Press enter \c"
        read yn
        done
    done
```

Caution

It may be wise not to use the second and fourth command
lines. I have experienced instances where, when these colors
are used and the application sends the sequence to bold, the
characters and the screen misbehave. The screen may start
flashing or some other strange behavior may occur. The
second line is the bold of the first, the fourth line is the bold
of the third, and so on. It seems that the bold of something
bolded isn't defined.

sh

sh starts the Bourne shell. The Bourne shell is one of many
command interpreters available under UNIX. A shell's job is
to take the command line you enter, check its syntax, parse
it, and pass it to the kernel in a manner the kernel can
understand. sh also is a programming language of sorts; it
provides all the control structures found in most high-level
languages. It lacks, however, floating-point math, and robust
file-reading tools.

Because sh is such a powerful utility, only the basics are
discussed here.

Syntax

```
    sh [flags] args
```

Argument or Option	Description
args	What you supply for *args* varies based on what flags you supplied. The common usage is the name of a shell script, or the name of a shell script and arguments to that script.

Messages

```
-c: bad option(s)
```

You invoked a shell with an option it didn't understand. *c* is replaced with the bad option.

```
script: script: cannot open
```

You asked sh to run a script that doesn't exist, or you don't have permissions to read the file.

Examples

```
sh
```

Invokes a new shell. You may now work in this shell, changing directories, setting environment variables, and so on. When you return to the original shell by pressing Ctrl-d or typing exit, you are returned to the directory from which you started the new shell, and any environment variables you changed are returned to their former values. Applications sometime let you run a UNIX command from the application. Entering sh as the command gives you a subshell to work in, letting you enter an entire series of commands.

```
sh install.prog
```

Runs an installation script.

```
EDITOR=/usr/bin/emacs; export EDITOR
```

Sets the environment variable EDITOR to a popular public
domain editor called Micro-Emacs. Applications can access
variables, such as EDITOR and alter their behavior based on
the variables' values.

```
while :
do
format /dev/rdsk/5h
done
```

This is a bit more tricky. A common task is to format flop-
pies, but no one wants to type in the format command repeatedly. You can use the programming capabilities of sh by
using a while loop. The commands listed on the lines between do and done are executed as long as the last line in
between while and do returns a zero value. : always returns
zero value, so this loop executes forever. When you're done
formatting all the disks, press the interrupt key (usually the
Delete key on the console).

```
while :
do
echo "Next floppy? \c"
read yn
tar xvf /dev/rdsk/5h
done
```

A more complex example introduces the echo and read commands of sh. This example is useful when the software product you just bought has a bunch of floppy disks that have to
be extracted, and you have to complete the repetitive task of
typing tar as many as 20 times. echo prompts the on-screen
message of Next Floppy without moving the cursor to the
next line (\c). The read command pauses for you to enter
something and stores the result in the made-up variable yn.
Simply pressing enter at the prompt causes tar to begin
extracting the files. When you're done, you can press the
interrupt key.

See also

csh, cd, env, tar

shutdown

UNIX is an operating system which has to be told that you want to turn it off. You can't just turn off the power on a UNIX system; well you can, but you're going to wish you hadn't. shutdown lets you control when the shutdown will take place, and it notifies the users on a regular basis. shutdown safely brings the system to a point where the power can be turned off.

Syntax

```
shutdown [flags] su
```

Argument or Option	Description
su	After the system goes through the shutdown process, it enters single-user mode without completely shutting down the system.

Flags

Argument or Option	Description
-y	Without this flag set, shutdown prompts you if you want to shut the system down. This forces a yes response to that question, and you are not asked if you want to shut down.
-gtime	Specifies the grace period before the shutdown occurs. time is expressed as hh:mm where hh is the number of hours, and mm is the number of minutes to wait before shutting down.

(continues)

Argument or Option	Description
-f*mesg*	Specifies the message to write to the users' terminals that the system will be shutting down. *mesg* must be enclosed in double quotation marks (-f"shutdown soon").
-F*mesgfile*	Specifies that the message to send to the users' terminals is found in the file *mesgfile*.

Notes

shutdown can only be run by the super user. Messages are sent to the users' terminals at intervals based on the amount of time left till the shutdown. The following table shows this:

Time remaining	Message sent every...
More than 1 hour	hour
More than 15 minutes	15 minutes
More than 1 minute	minute

Messages

    shutdown: not found

If you get this message, it is probably because /etc isn't in your search path (PATH), which means you probably aren't the super user. You can't run shutdown unless you are the super user.

    device busy

Part of the shutdown process is to unmount all the file systems. If a file system is still in use at the time of the shutdown, then umount complains. This situation arises if a user ignored the messages about the shutdown and was using one of the mounted file systems.

Examples

```
shutdown
```

This is the simplest way to invoke shutdown. With this approach, shutdown prompts you to see if you really wanted to shut down. It then asks for the grace period and whether you want to send a message other than the default.

```
shutdown -y -g1: -F/etc/shutdown.msg su
```

This line tells shutdown not to prompt for confirmation on the shutdown that will take place in one hour. shutdown sends the contents of the file /etc/shutdown.msg to all the users logged on the system. When the hour is up, the system will go through the shutdown process and go to single-user mode.

See also

wall, haltsys, reboot

sleep

Suspends execution for an interval of time.

Syntax

```
sleep seconds
```

Argument or Option	Description
seconds	Specifies the number of seconds to sleep. This must be an integer.

Note

sleep is not guaranteed to wake up exactly the number of seconds specified.

Examples

```
while :
do
    date
    sleep 60
done
```

Shows the date every 60 seconds.

sort

Enables you to sort and merge text files. Sorts may be based on character fields or numeric fields, and multiple sort keys may be specified.

Syntax

```
sort [flags] files
```

Argument or Option	Description
files	An optional list of files to be sorted or merged. If no files are specified or - is used as the file name, then the standard input is read.

Flags

Argument or Option	Description
-c	Checks to see if the files are sorted. If they are, then no output is generated.

Argument or Option	Description
-m	Merges the specified files. It is assumed that the files are already sorted.
-u	Makes sure only unique lines go to the output. The uniqueness of a line is based on the sort keys.
-o*file*	Specifies the output file name. This may be the same as one of the input file names. Normally, the output of sort is the standard output.
-y*kmem*	The amount of memory, expressed in kilobytes, to use for the sort area. Normally, sort grows in memory size to satisfy its needs. This flag can specify an amount known to be optimal for this sort.
-z*reclen*	The length of the longest line of the output. Normally, sort determines the longest line while sorting the input files. However, the -m and -c options may need the *reclen* to avoid abnormal termination.
-d	Sorts in dictionary order. Only letters, digits, and blanks are used for ordering.
-f	"Folds," or changes, lowercase letters to uppercase for sort purposes.
-i	Ignores nonprintable characters in the sort keys.
-M	Treats sort key as if it was a month. JAN less than FEB that is less than MAR, and so on. This implies the -b flag.

(continues)

Argument or Option	Description
-n	Specifies a key is a numeric key; implies the -b flag.
-r	Reverses the sort (descending).
-t*fld-sep*	Specifies that the field separator is the character *fld-sep*, not tabs or blanks.
-b	Ignores leading blanks when determining the value of the sort keys.
+*keybeg*	Specifies that the sort key starts at field number *keybeg*. Fields start counting at zero; the fifth field is a 4. *keybeg* accepts the format M.NF, where M is the field number, and N is the character offset within that field. The absence of .N assumes zero. F may be any of the following flags: b, d, f, i, n, or r, which have the same meanings as described previously except that they apply only to this key.
-*keyend*	Specifies on what field number the key ends, and follows the same format rules of +*keybeg*. If no ending field number is specified, the end of the line is assumed.

Notes

When multiple keys are used, the keys specified later in the command line are compared when the earlier ones are equal. For example:

```
sort +2 -3  +5 -6
```

the key defined by character positions 5 -6 are compared only when the the key defined by positions 2 -3 does not define a uniq record. All comparisons are governed by the locale of the system; this allows support for international usage.

Because sort distinguishes records by looking for the newline character, the command is not suitable for binary files.

Messages

```
sort: invalid use of command line options
```

You specified a flag sort doesn't understand.

```
sort: can't open filename
```

You specified a file name that doesn't exist.

```
sort: can't create filename
```

You specified the -o option with a file name in a directory for which you don't have permissions to write, or the file name exists and you don't have write permissions.

Examples

```
ps -e ¦ sort
```

Because the first column of ps is the PID number, this gives you the processes running on the system in PID order.

```
ps -e ¦ sort +3
```

Because the last column of ps is the name of the command, this gives a list of the processes running by command name.

```
ps -e ¦ sort -u +3
```

Strips out any duplicate process names.

```
ps -e ¦ sort -r +2 -3
```

The third column is the CPU time the process has had. This reverses the sort, pushing the CPU hogs at the top.

See also

uniq, join, ps

spell

Checks spelling of a text file. An option to add and remove words from the dictionary also exists.

Syntax

```
spell [flags] +userdict filelist
```

Argument or Option	Description
+userdict	A file containing a list of words that, although not found in the system dictionary, should be considered correctly spelled. userdict should have one word per line.
filelist	The files to read and spell check. If no files are specified, spell reads from the standard input.

Message

```
cat: cannot open myfile: No such file or directory
```

This message means you tried to spell check the file myfile and that file did not exist.

Flags

Argument or Option	Description
-v	All words not literally in the dictionary appear along with a list of possible spellings.

Argument or Option	Description
-b	Use the British dictionary.
-l	spell supports the troff macros .so and .nx. These are used to chain files together to create a complete document. Normally, spell does not follow the path if the path name begins with /usr /lib. The -l causes spell to look at these files as well.
-i	Causes spell to ignore all chaining requests.

Example

```
spell letter-to-mom
```

Examines the file letter-to-mom and displays the misspelled words.

split

Breaks up a text file into smaller pieces. Periodically, files become too large to load into an editor or some other utility. split lets you handle the file in more manageable pieces.

Syntax

```
split -numlines file tagname
```

Argument or Option	Description
-numlines	Specifies the number of lines to include in each piece.

(continues)

Argument or Option	Description
file	The file to split into smaller pieces. If left blank or - is used, then standard input is read.
tagname	By default, split builds the output pieces by creating the following files: *x*aa, then *x*ab, then *x*ac, and so on. *tagname*, if specified, replaces the *x* in the previous list thus building the list: *tagname*aa, *tagname*ab, *tagname*ac, and so on.

Note

There must be enough room for two copies of the file in the current file system.

Message

```
cannot open input
```

You supplied spilt with a file name that doesn't exist.

Examples

```
split -1000 letter-to-dad dadletter
```

Apparently the previous letter-to-dad was a large one. This line breaks up that letter into 1,000 line pieces. The output files are dadletteraa, dadletterab, and so on.

```
cat dadletter* >letter-to-dad
```

Takes all the pieces and puts them back together again into the file letter-to-dad.

See also

cat

strings

Extracts the printable strings from an object module.

Syntax

```
strings [flags] filelist
```

Argument or Option	Description
filelist	A space separated list of file names to be examined for strings.

Flags

Argument or Option	Description
-	Normally, strings examines only the initialized data space of an object file. - tells strings to examine the entire file.
-o	Shows the byte offset in the file where the string is found.
-number	Normally, the length of a valid string is four printable characters in a row. This option allows you to control the minimum length of a string.

Example

```
strings /bin/ls
```

Shows all strings in the program ls

See also

od, hd

stty

Sets the terminal device driver line controls. stty provides many options to control the tty driver. You may set the character size, parity, baud rate, input preprocessing of special characters, and output processing of special characters.

Syntax

```
stty -a -g settings
```

Argument or Option	Description
-a	Shows all current settings of the currently logged on terminal. Normally, stty gives a reduced version of all the settings. stty actually reads from the terminal driver. So, if you want to see what the terminal settings are for another tty, just redirect the input to stty (see example that follows).
-g	Like -a but produces 12 hexadecimal numbers separated by colons. This output is suitable for input to stty.
settings	The settings may either be the output of a previous -g flag, or a series of stty commands.

Note

It is important to understand that stty changes how the system's tty driver behaves in reference to what your terminal is physically set to. There are two ends to having a terminal communicate: the physical settings on the device, and how the system thinks it should talk to the device. If these aren't equal, then the communication breaks down. stty only affects how the system thinks the device is talking. You use stty to enable the system to talk to tty devices with varying communication needs.

Message

```
/dev/console: cannot open
```

You tried to manipulate a port you don't have permissions to work with.

Examples

```
stty -a
```

Shows all the settings on this tty.

```
stty -a </dev/tty02
```

Shows you all the settings on the second console.

```
(^-J)stty sane(^-J)
```

Occasionally a program crashes leaving your terminal in a state in which it doesn't seem to be accepting your input. In this case, entering the preceding command returns your terminal to a usable state. Note that the notation (Ctrl-j) indicates that you hold down the Control key while pressing the J key. Do not type in the parentheses or the Enter key.

su

Substitutes another user id for yours. Enables you to become someone else on the system so that you can access their files; you need to know their password to do this. su is commonly used to become the super user (root).

Syntax

```
su - user arguments
```

Argument or Option	Description
-	Logs you on as this user, running through /etc/profile and her .profile file.
user	The user you want to become. If left blank, root is assumed.
arguments	Any arguments specified are passed to the program invoked by the shell. A common use is to specify -c followed by a command to execute. Runs that command as if you were that user and then returns. You become that user only for the time it takes to execute the command.

Rule

The super user may change to any other user without having that person's password, but if you wanted to change to another user you would need his or her password.

Messages

```
Unknown id: baduserid
```

You asked to become a user that doesn't exist on your system. *baduserid* is replaced by the user you tried to become.

```
Sorry
```

You did not enter the correct password when prompted.

Example

```
su - frank
```

You become the user frank and go through the login process as if you had logged on as frank.

```
su - accounting -c "close-month"
```

Here you become the accounting user to run a program called "close-month."

swconfig

Lists the software packages installed with the custom utility.

Syntax

```
swconfig -a -p
```

Argument or Option	Description
-a	Shows all information available; a more extensive listing.
-p	Shows the software packages.

Examples

```
swconfig
```

Gives you a concise report of the applications installed, the release number, and indicates whether the application is installed.

```
swconfig -a
```

Gives a much more thorough report.

See also

custom, hwconfig

sync

Writes the current disk image held in the system's disk I/O buffers to the hard disk. You have to make sure that the buffers are written before you shut the machine down; otherwise, the disk does not have a correct image of the information written to it. However, because both shutdown and haltsys do a sync, the need to use sync is limited.

Syntax

```
sync
```

Example

```
sync
```

Causes the system disk buffers to be written.

See also

haltsys, shutdown

tabs

Sets the tab stops on the terminal.

Syntax

```
tabs tabstops -Tterm +mlmrgn
```

Flags

Argument or Option	Description
-T*term*	Specifies what terminal type obtains the codes used to program the terminal's tab stops. If *term* isn't specified, the environment variable TERM is used.
+m*lmrgn*	Specifies the left margin. *tabstops* is expressed relative to *lmrgn*.
tabstops	Specifies the tab stops; can have any of the following four constructs:

	-*code*	A predefined set of common programming languages' conventional tab settings. If you don't use these languages or don't like the settings, this option isn't very helpful. See your reference guide for specifics.
	-*every-n*	Makes the tab stop *every-n* + 1 characters.
	-*list*	A comma separated list of tab stops. If a number, other than the first one, is preceded by a plus sign (+), the number is considered an increment of the first.
	-*file*	Specifies that the tab stops are in file *file* and conforms to the rules outlined in fspec(F).

Rule

The terminal must support host-set tab stops.

Messages

```
illegal tabs
```

You used the *list* form to specify the tab stops, and this list is not in the correct order.

```
illegal increment
```

Message appears if, using the *list* form, you did not specify the increment value correctly.

```
unknown tab code
```

You attempted to specify a predefined tab stop that doesn't exist.

Examples

```
tabs -4
```

Sets the tab stops at 5, 9, 13, 17, and so on.

```
tabs 1,5,9,13,17
```

Performs the same action as the previous command for the first five tab stops.

```
tabs 1,+4
```

This command accomplishes the same thing as the previous command.

tail

Enables you to view the end of a text file or track the growth of a text file.

Syntax

tail *beg-offset* -f *file*

Argument or Option	Description
beg-offset	The offset within the file to begin viewing. If *beg-offset* is preceded with a -, then the offset is relative to the end of the file. If a + is used, then the offset is relative to the beginning of the file. The following qualifiers may be used to specify *beg-offset*'s unit of measure:
	b The offset is expressed in blocks.
	l The offset is expressed in lines; this is the default.
	c The offset is expressed in characters.
	If *beg-offset* is left blank then 10 lines are assumed.
-f	When this option is used, and the input is not standard input, tail monitors the growth of the file. This is an endless loop of output and has to be terminated with the interrupt key.
file	The name of the file of which you want to view the end, or track its growth. If *file* is left blank, the standard input is used.

Message

tail: illegal option -- *option*

You tried to invoke tail with an option other then -f.

Examples

```
tail letter-to-dad
```

Looks at the final 10 lines of letter-to-dad.

```
tail -10c letter-to-dad
```

Looks at the last 10 characters of letter-to-dad.

```
tail +10 letter-to-dad
```

Begins showing letter-to-dad after the first 10 lines are read.

```
tail -f growing-file ¦ more
```

Assuming a file called growing-file was built by some other
process, this shows you what is built so far and what is generated on an ongoing basis. Pipe the output through the pager
more in case it generates too fast to view on-screen.

See also

more, pg

tar

Used to create tape archives (backups of your file system) or
saves and restores files to and from an archive medium.

Syntax

```
tar action[flags] flag-args filelist
```

Argument or Option	Description
action	Specifies what action to take on the archive. *action* may be one of the following:
	c Creates a new archive, or overwrites an existing one.
	r Writes the files named in *filelist* to the end of the archive, appending the existing archive.
	t Gives a table of contents of the archive.
	u Updates the archive. Add the files named in *filelist* to the end of the archive if they aren't found in the archive or they have been modified since the last write. (May take quite a bit of time.)
	x Extracts the files or directories named in *filelist*.
filelist	The list of files to manipulate may contain wild cards (see Caution later in this entry). If *filelist* is a directory, then that directory is recursively traversed matching all files within that directory's substructure.
flag-args	When a flag requires an argument, the arguments are delayed until after all the flags have been specified. Then the arguments are listed on the command line in the same order as the flags.

Flags

Argument or Option	Description
key	A number between 0 and 9999. This number is a key to the file /etc/default/tar that specifies default options for the device name, blocking factor, device size, and whether the device is a tape.
b	Specifies the blocking factor. May be any integer between 1 and 20. The default is 1. Only use this with raw tape/floppy devices. Requires an argument.
f	Specifies the file name to be used as the archive. May be a regular file or a special character device (for example, /dev/rdsk/5h for a high- density floppy). If - is used, then standard input is read from or written to depending on the action specified. (You cannot pipe a *filelist* to tar as with cpio, or pcpio.) Requires an argument.
l	Tells tar to display an error message if it can't resolve all the links to a file. Normally, tar is silent about archiving a set of files when not all the links are specified. Used only with the c, r, and u actions
m	Tells tar not to restore the modification times. The modification time is the time of extraction.
v	Places tar into verbose mode. The file names are displayed on the terminal as tar processes them. When used with the t option, tar gives you a listing similar to the long listing of the ls command.

Argument or Option	Description
w	Causes tar to wait for you to respond with a Y or an N before taking action on the file. Actually, any response starting with the letter Y means yes, and any other response means no. Not valid with the t action.
F	The next argument is a file that holds a list of files to be manipulated.
k	The next argument is the size in kilobytes of the device. This enables tar to know when it has filled up the device and when it has to prompt for the next media.
n	This tells tar that the device is not a tape drive. For floppy devices, this allows tar to seek to the files it wants.
A	Changes all absolute file names to relative file names.

Notes

When listing the file names, you have to be sure you use absolute or relative path names. Files are extracted from the archive in the same way they were created. Furthermore, if you request only a single file to be extracted, you must specify that file name on the command line the same way it was created. For example, suppose you created an archive using the following:

```
tar cvf /dev/rdsk/5h /usr/sue
```

This creates an archive of all the files in the directory hierarchy /usr/sue. If you want to get back a file called letters-to-dad, you have to enter the following:

```
tar xf /dev/rdsk/5h /usr/sue/letters-to-dad
```

If you only specify `letters-to-dad` in the *filelist*, `tar` does not find the file.

Messages

> `tar: tape write error`

This usually means one of several things: You don't have a floppy or tape in the drive; you have filled up the floppy or tape; the tape is write-protected; or you need to clean the drive.

> `tar: tape read error`

This usually means you don't have a floppy/tape in the drive, the door isn't properly shut to the drive, or you have bad media.

> `tar: directory checksum error`

This usually means one of two things: You have specified the wrong media type for the floppy or tape drive, or the tape has to be rewound. Specifying the wrong media type is a common error. Users have been known to place a 360K floppy disk in the drive and then access it with the `/dev/rdsk/5h` device.

Example

> `tar cvf /dev/rdsk/5h .`

Notes

If no device is specified for `tar`, it uses a default device— usually the floppy drive.

Creates an archive on the high-density floppy drive of the current directory showing all the file names it came across.

> `tar xvf /dev/rdsk/5h`

Extracts all the files found on the floppy disk showing you the names of the files it came across.

```
tar cvbf 20 /dev/rdsk/5h /usr/sue
```

Demonstrates the syntax involved when combining flags that require arguments. This line is an example of creating an archive of sue's home directory, using a blocking factor of 20 and placing the archive on the high-density floppy disk.

```
tar cf - /usr/sue ¦ wc -c
```

The value of this particular command is questionable. However, it shows how to use the - to send the output to standard output. An archive of sue's home directory was created, piping the output through wc to get a count of the characters. This tells you how big the archive is.

Caution

Special devices are not placed on the archive.

Caution

Wild cards may be used in *filelist*. However, the tar command doesn't do any wild-card expansion. The shell does the expansion and passes the result to tar. This can be a problem for novice users who have deleted files and then want to extract them from the archive. Because the file doesn't exist on the file system, the shell can't expand the wild cards to match the nonexistent files. To illustrate this, suppose you had a series of files that all ended with the letters .ltr. You can create the archive of the entire directory, not just the .ltr files, using the following:

```
tar cf /dev/rdsk/5h .
```

After realizing that you messed up all the files ending with .ltr, you can extract them from the archive with the following:

```
tar xf /dev/rdsk/5h *.ltr
```

This then restores the fouled .ltr files. However, if the files were deleted, tar does not find any files to extract. It does not find anymore than the following ls command does.

```
ls *.ltr
```

In a case where the files have been deleted, you have to specify each one in full without the use of wild cards. Alternatively, a pass with the t option redirected to a file can be used.

```
tar tf /dev/rdsk/5h >list.tmp
```

Then use the following to get back all the files ending in .lst:

```
tar xf /dev/rdsk/5h 'grep ".lst$" list.tmp'
```

See also

tar, cpio, pcpio, backup, restore, xbackup, xrestore ls, wc, grep

tee

Splits the output in a pipeline to one or more files. This enables you to capture what is going to standard output and place that output into a file and still allow the output to flow through standard output.

Syntax

```
tee [flags] filelist
```

Argument or Option	Description
filelist	The space separated list of files into which you want to capture the output.

Flags

Argument or Option	Description
-i	Causes tee to ignore interrupts.
-a	The files in *filelist* are appended with the output, instead of overwritten.
-u	The output through tee is unbuffered.

Example

```
l ¦ tee listing ¦ more
```

Places a copy of the file listing generated by l in the file listing, while you view the listing through the pager more.

See also

l, more

test

Most commonly used in if and while statements. if and while are sh control constructs used when programming in the Bourne shell. test returns a zero exit status if what it tested is true.

Syntax

```
test expression

[ expression ]
```

Argument or Option	Description
expression	This is the expression that test tests. The following may be used to build a valid expression:

-r *file*		True if *file* has read permissions.
-w *file*		True if *file* has write permissions.
-x *file*		True if *file* has execute permissions.
-f *file*		True if *file* is a regular file.
-d *file*		True if *file* is a directory.
-b *file*		True if *file* exists and is a block special file.
-c *file*		True if *file* is a block special file.
-u *file*		True if *file* has the set-user-ID flag set.
-g *file*		True if *file* has the set-group-ID set.
-k *file*		True if *file* has the sticky-bit set.
-s *file*		True if *file* has a files size greater than zero.
-t *fd*		True if the file with file descriptor *fd* is opened and associated with terminal device. The default *fd* is 1.
-z *str*		True if the length of the string *str* is zero.

Argument or Option	Description	
	-n *str*	True if the length of the string *str* is nonzero.
	str1 = *str2*	
		True if string *str1* equals the string *str2*.
	str1 != *str2*	
		True if string *str1* doesn't equal the string *str2*.
	str	True if the string *str* is not a null string.
	int1 -eq *int2*	
		True if the integer *int1* equals the integer *int2*. The following also may be used instead of -eq.
	-ne	not equal
	-gt	greater than
	-ge	greater than or equal
	-lt	less than
	-le	less than or equal
	!	Negates the expression.
	-a	A logical AND.
	-o	A logical OR.
	( )	Used for grouping.

Note

All the file-oriented tests are false if the file doesn't exist.

Message

```
test: argument expected
```

test was expecting something, and you didn't give it. This can be caused by several factors: You gave it an invalid argument; or quite typically, you were testing an environment variable, and it wasn't set to anything. It didn't expand in the command line and test expected an argument there.

Examples

```
if [ -f letter-to-dad ]
    then
    echo "letter-to-dad exists"
fi
```

Tests to see if the file letter-to-dad exists and is a regular file.

```
if [ -f letter-to-dad -a -f letter-to-mom ]
    then
    echo "both letters written"
fi
```

Tests to see that letter-to-dad and letter-to-mom have been written.

Tip

The second form [*expression*] is useful for readability. [is actually a program name found on the file system that is linked to test.

time

Determines how long a program takes to execute.

Syntax

```
time command
```

Argument or Option	Description
command	The command you want to time.

Notes

time reports three different times:

Argument or Option	Description
real	The total elapsed time since you invoked the command. This is sometimes referred to as "wall clock" time, because it is the time that has elapsed on the clock on your wall.
user	This is the amount of time actually spent on the CPU outside sys time.
sys	This is the amount of time spent in the kernel; the amount of time spent fulfilling system requests.

The total CPU time is user + sys time. The difference between this and real time is the amount of time the CPU spends on other tasks.

Example

```
time compress letter-to-dad
```

Reports the amount of time it takes to compress the file let-ter-to-dad.

touch

Changes the access and modification times of a file, or creates a new file with specified times.

Syntax

```
touch [flags] MMDDhhmmYY filelist
```

Argument or Option	Description
MMDDhhmmYY	This is the time to which to set the file. The format is as follows:
	MM The month
	DD The day
	hh The hour
	mm The minute
	YY The year
filelist	A space separated list of the files that you want to have the specified time.

Flags

Argument or Option	Description
-a	The specified time changes the access time of the specified files.
-m	Same as -a, but for modified time.
-c	If a file in *filelist* doesn't exist, then this flag tells touch not to create it.

Notes

The flags -am are the default. You cannot modify the creation time of a file. (The term *creation time* is a bit misleading. The creation time is not really the time the file was created, it is better thought of as when the i-node information changed. When the file size changed, the mode changed, the owner changed, and so on.)

Message

    touch: illegal option -- *badoption*

You tried to specify a flag *badoption* which touch doesn't understand. (*badoption* is substituted with the flag you supplied.)

Examples

    touch letter-to-dad

Sets the modification and access times of letter-to-dad to the current date.

    touch 0101120191 letter-to-dad

Sets the modification and access times of letter-to-dad to 01/01/91 at 12:01 p.m.

See also

date

tr

tr translates or maps characters in a file from one form to another. For example, you can use tr to change all tabs to spaces. This command enables you to do some rather robust character handling with a somewhat simple structure.

Syntax

tr [*flags*] *from-string to-string*

Argument or Option	Description
from-string	This is the string of characters from which to map; the characters you want translated. The following special notations may be used and repeated:
	[c_1-c_n] This specifies a range of characters from c1 to c*n*.
	[c**n*] This specifies that character c repeats *n* times. *n* may be zero or left blank, which assumes a huge number of the character c. This is useful for padding the *to-string* (see Note later in this entry).
octal	Specifies the octal value of a character. This is useful for manipulating the nonprintable characters (control characters).

Argument or Option	Description
to-string	This is the string of characters to map into; the character to which the from-string translates. The special notations noted previously may be used here, as well.

Flags

Argument or Option	Description
-c	Normally, tr substitutes the characters found in from-string with the characters found in to-string, with the output showing the original contents of the file with the substitution applied. This option restricts the output to the characters specified in from-string and effectively appends the characters in to-string.
-d	Deletes the characters specified in from-string.
-s	Strips repeated characters generated in the output by those specified in to-string, leaving only one of the repeated characters in the output.

Note

The to-string must be the same number of characters as the from-string.

Message

```
bad string
```

This is usually a case where the number of characters in
from-string and *to-string* aren't equal.

Examples

```
tr -d "\015\032" <dosfile >unixfile
```

This is one way of translating DOS text files into a format
more suitable in UNIX. It deletes the carriage returns and the
DOS end-of-file marker (^Z).

```
tr -s "\015\032" "[\012*]" <dosfile >unixfile
```

This is a significantly more complicated way of accomplish-
ing the same task as the previous example. However, it demonstrates two features of tr. In this example, you replace all
the carriage returns and end-of-file markers with the UNIX
newline character. The -s strips the duplicate newlines,
producing only one. *to-string* uses the "padding" option
described previously to ensure that the lengths of the two
strings are equal.

Tip

Enclose *from-string* and *to-string* in quotation marks as
shown in the examples to ensure that the special meaning of
any characters recognized by the shell is escaped and passed
to tr rather than expanded by the shell.

Caution

The range notation may be used with the characters representing the digits as well, such as 0-9. However, such notation refers strictly to the digits themselves and not the value
they may represent. You cannot use this to replace all tens
with nines, as ten is two digits and nine is only one digit.

See also

ed

true

Returns a zero exit status, which in the shell is what means true. This command is useful when programing in the shell to create continuous loops.

Syntax

```
true
```

Examples

```
while true
do
     format /dev/rdsk/5h
done
```

Formatting floppy disks is one of the rituals of computer use. Rather than typing the format command repeatedly, have the computer do the repetitive work for you. When you're done with the stack of floppy disks, you can just hit the interrupt key at the format's prompt to kill the loop.

Tip

The character : in the Bourne shell gives the same results as true and doesn't require the execution of a program.

See also

sh

tty

Reports the currently logged on terminal device name, or tests if standard input is a terminal.

Syntax

```
tty -s
```

Argument or Option	Description
-s	This option causes tty to test if the standard input is a terminal device or not. No output is generated. The result code is set to zero if standard input is a terminal, one if it is not.

Message

```
not a tty
```

This message displays when you try to invoke tty, you haven't used the -s flag, and the standard input is not a terminal.

Examples

```
tty
```

Simply reports the terminal's device name.

```
if tty -s
    then
    echo "This is a terminal"
fi
```

Tests if the standard input is a terminal or not.

umask

Specifies the default permissions of your files, or reports the current defaults.

Syntax

umask *mask*

Argument or Option	Description
mask	The mask that is applied when generating the permissions for the files you create. If left blank, umask reports the current setting. *mask* is composed of three digits. The digits represent the permissions for the owner of the file, (that's you), the group, and the rest of the world. The mask is called a mask because the value specified is actually masked at the bit level to generate the permissions. However, if you don't think in this way, (most people don't), then simply think of mask as the permissions you don't want to give.

0	You don't want to restrict any permissions.
1	You want to restrict execute permissions.
2	You want to restrict write permission.
4	You want to restrict read permissions.

Adding any of these numbers together restricts the combination of the permissions. A 7 restricts all permissions.

Examples

    umask

Reports the current mask setting.

    umask 000

Gives complete access to everyone on the system to every file you create.

    umask 022

Gives you complete permissions on the files you create. However, everyone else is only able to read and execute those files.

    umask 007

Gives you and the people in your group complete permissions and doesn't allow anyone else to do anything.

See also

    chmod

umnt

See mnt.

uname

Reports the system name and other catalogue information.

Syntax

    uname [flags]

Flags

Argument or Option	Description
-s	Reports the system name. This is the default.
-n	Reports the node name of the system. This is used in communications.
-r	Reports the release number of the operating system.
-v	Shows the version number of the operating system.
-m	Reports the machine hardware name.
-a	Reports all the above information, equivalent to -mvrns.

Message

uname: illegal option -- *badoption*

You invoked uname with an option it doesn't recognize.

Example

uname

Reports the system name of the currently logged-on machine.

uncompress

See compress.

uniq

Strips out lines that are identical, producing only one unique line.

Syntax

```
uniq [flags] input output
```

Argument or Option	Description
input	The name of the file from which to read; if left blank, the standard input is read.
output	The name of the file to create with the results of the uniq command. If left blank, then standard output is used. If specified, *output* must not be the same as *input*.

Flags

Argument or Option	Description
-u	Causes uniq to output only those lines that aren't repeated.
-d	Causes uniq to output only those lines that were repeated—but only one copy of them.
-c	Produces a report with the left column as the number of times the line repeated and then the line itself.
-*fields*	When doing the comparison for uniqueness, the first *fields* count of fields is skipped. Fields are separated by tabs or spaces.

Argument or Option	Description
+*chars*	After skipping any specified fields, also skips *chars* number of characters.

Notes

The default operation is to output all the lines in the input file, but with only one copy of any repeated lines.

uniq assumes the input file is already sorted.

Examples

```
who ¦ cut -d" " -f1 ¦ uniq
```

Shows a list of users currently logged on the system; if anyone is logged on more than once, you see them once.

```
who ¦ cut -d" " -f1 ¦ uniq -d
```

This is a slight twist on the previous command. This is an example showing those who logged on more than once.

```
who ¦ cut -d" " -f1 ¦ uniq -u
```

Shows only those who have not logged on more than once.

```
who ¦ cut -d" " -f1 ¦ uniq -c
```

With this command you get a list of each user on the system and a count of the number of times they are logged on.

See also

sort

unpack

A companion command to pack. unpack reverses the process of pack, restoring the file to its original form.

Syntax

unpack *filelist*

Argument or Option	Description
filelist	The space delimited list of files to unpack. You don't have to specify the .z, as this is assumed.

Messages

unpack: *filename*.z: cannot open

You've asked unpack to unpack a file that doesn't exist with a .z appended.

unpack: *filename*.z: not it packed format

A filename with .z appended existed, but it is not in packed format. The .z on the end of the file is a coincidence; it didn't mean the file was packed.

Example

unpack letter-to-dad

Apparently you wrote a rather large letter to dad and had packed it to reduce its storage requirements. This command unpacks it, presumably to modify or print it.

See also

pack

uucp

uucp stands for UNIX-to-UNIX copy. uucp enables you to copy files across a network to another UNIX machine. Typically, this network consists of asynchronous telephone lines.

Syntax

```
uucp [ flags ] source_list destination
```

Argument or Option	Description
source_list	A space separated list of files you want to copy.
destination	The destination name to which you copy. If multiple source files are given, this must be a directory name.

source_list and destination can be preceded by an optional machine name followed by a "bang" or exclamation mark (!). The following syntax is valid:

```
machine_name!file_name
```

Wild cards (*, ?, and [ ]) are expanded on the appropriate machine. When wild cards are used for the file_name on a remote machine, the request is sent, processed by that machine, and the files are sent later. The actual transfer is not guaranteed to take place at the initial connection.

The special notation of ~user can be used as part of file_name. This tells uucp to look for the file in user's home directory (for example, uucp mfg!~frank/daily_sales . This gets the file daily_sales from frank's home directory on the machine mfg and copies it to the current directory of the local machine). When using this notation for the destination, and when ~user on the remote machine is not accessible by uucp, the file is placed in /usr/spool/uucppublic and the user is notified by way of mail.

The notation of ~/ also can be used as shorthand for /usr /spool/uucppublic.

If a file being transferred is an executable program, then those executable permissions are preserved across the transmission. The owner of the file on the remote machine becomes uucp and the permissions of read and write for owner, group, and other are set.

Flags

Argument or Option	Description
-c	Does not copy the file to be transferred to the spool directory before transferring to the remote machine. This is the default.
-C	Copies the file to the spool directory before transferring. (This option enables you to delete the file from the local system after the uucp request is made.)
-d	Makes all necessary directories for the copy (default).
-f	Does not make the directories.
-ggrade	A single character to prioritize the order of transfer for this request. The lower the ASCII value of grade, the earlier in the connection the request is carried out. (For example, if you had 10 files to transfer you can give each a different grade to change the order in which they transfer.)
-j	Shows the job number this request is assigned by uucp. This number is suitable for use with uustat to check the status of the job.
-m	Sends mail to you when the copy is completed.

Argument or Option	Description
-n*user*	Sends mail to the user *user* on the remote machine when the copy is completed.
-r	Queues up the request, but does not actually start the transfer.
-s*file_name*	Logs the status of the transfer to the file *file_name*.
-x*debug_level*	Debugging levels 0-9 are available. Each number gives more detailed debugging information on the status of the connection; 9 gives you the most information.

Rules

uucp can't connect to a remote machine until the following files are properly set up. (See your system's administrators guide for help):

File	Description
/usr/lib/uucp/Devices	The list of valid modem ports on which to dial out.
/usr/lib/uucp/Systems	The list of machines your machine knows how to call, what modems to use to call, when to call, the phone number to call, and a chat script to send the remote machine's login process.
/usr/lib/uucp/Permissions	The list of machines you now want to call you or send you information if you call them. This contains the list of commands these machines can

(continues)

File	Description
	request your machine to run, the list of directories from which it can read or write, and several other layers of security issues.
/etc/systemid	The name of the local machine for uucp purposes.

If no machine name is given for either the source or destination than uucp simply uses cp to copy the file locally. You can use uucp and not cp to copy local files.

uucp is a spooled process. That is, uucp takes your requests and executes them for you. You do not have to interact with or watch the file transfer take place. The machine that you want the file from can be called at night to save on phone rates.

Messages

```
can't get status for file /usr/acct/benah/ben
uucp failed partially: 0 file(s) sent; 1 error(s)
```

You tried to copy a file on the local machine that doesn't exist. In this case that file name is /usr/acct/benah/ben.

```
bad system: frank
uucp failed completely (11)
```

You tried to send a file to, or receive a file from, a machine that doesn't exist in your /usr/lib/uucp/Systems file; in this case that machine is frank.

```
uucp: illegal option -- Q
unknown flag -Q
```

You tried to give uucp an option flag that uucp doesn't understand; in this example it is an uppercase Q.

```
usage uucp from ... to
uucp failed completely (2)
```

You didn't give enough arguments, uucp needs both a source and a destination.

Examples

```
uucp -m  -j mfg!~/daily_sales mfg!~/invt_lvl .
```

Calls up the machine mfg and gets two files from /usr/spool /uucppublic: daily_sales and invt_lvl. You are mailed when the transfer is complete and the uucp job number is shown on-screen after you execute the command.

```
uucp -nfrank -m my_file mfg!~frank
```

Example gets a file in the current directory called my_file and sends it to frank's home directory if it can be written to by uucp, otherwise it goes to /usr/spool/uucppublic. frank is notified when the file shows up, and you are mailed when the copy is complete.

vi

vi stands for visual ex. vi is the same editor as ex except it is full screen, and you are able to see the changes you make. vi is such a powerful tool that this discussion only provides rudimentary information on vi. If you want to work with vi, consult both the user's guide and user's reference provided with your system.

Syntax

```
vi filename

view filename

vedit filename
```

The three forms all invoke the same editor. The first form is the normal form. view invokes the editor in a read-only mode, thus enabling vi to act somewhat like the pagers more and pg; however, view can't be piped to. vedit places the editor in novice mode, which can be useful for beginners.

Argument or Option	Description
filename	This is the name of the file to edit.

The following are a few of the commands available in vi:

Command	What it does
Esc	Pressing the Escape key puts you back into command mode, allowing you to enter a new command.
r	Replaces one character
R	Unlimited replacement in the line
i	Insert mode
dd	Delete the line
x	Delete a character
$	End of the line
^	Beginning of the line
:x	Writes the file and exits vi
:q!	Quits vi without saving the file
/	Allows the entry of a search pattern

Example

    vi letter-to-dad

Starts vi to work on a letter to your dad.

See also

    ed

w

Reports who is logged on the system and what they are doing. It also reports how many users are on the system, how long the system has been up, and the load averages. The load averages are the average number of processes in the last 1, 5, and 15 minutes.

Syntax

    w [flags] users

Argument or Option	Description
users	A space separated list of users to which to limit the output of w. Normally, w reports all users.

Flags

Argument or Option	Description
-h	Does not show the header information. Normally, w prints a heading line showing the current date, how long the system has been up, the number of users currently logged on, and the load averages.
-l	The default; specifies the long format and produces the following columns:

<table>
<tr><td>User</td><td>The user logged on.</td></tr>
<tr><td>Tty</td><td>The terminal the user is on.</td></tr>
<tr><td>Login@</td><td>Indicates when the user logged on this terminal.</td></tr>
</table>

(continues)

Argument or Option	Description	
	Idle	The number of minutes the user hasn't typed anything at the terminal. This doesn't mean the processes on the terminal aren't doing something useful. It may be that the user launched a process that takes a long time to execute, but requires no interaction (for example, a large sort).
	JCPU	The cumulative CPU minutes used by all jobs run during this login session.
	PCPU	The number of CPU minutes the present process is taking.
	What	The name of the currently running process with its arguments.
-q	The quick output. Lists only the following from the table: User, Tty, Idle, and What.	
-t	Prints only the heading line; equivalent to uptime.	

Message

    w: illegal option -- badoption

You invoked w with an option/flag it doesn't support.

Examples

    w

Reports all possible information.

    w -t

Reports the uptime, number of users, and load average information.

    w frank sue

Reports information on the users frank and sue only.

See also

who, whodo, uptime, ps, finger

wall

Writes to all users currently logged on the system. This is a broadcast message.

Syntax

    wall

wall reads from standard input until an end-of-file (Ctrl-d) is reached. It then broadcasts this message to all users on the system.

Notes

You must be the super user to run wall and to override any write protection the users have. The wall executable is found in the /etc directory, and the system default does not enable regular users execute permissions.

Examples

```
wall
Please get off the system in 10 minutes^D
```

Invokes an interactive version of wall and types in a one line message ending with the end-of-file keystroke (Ctrl-d). The message doesn't go out until the end-of-file is encountered.

```
wall <shutdown-note
```

Redirects the file shutdown-note to wall and sends the contents of that file to all users.

See also

write

wc

Counts the number of characters, words, or lines in a file.

Syntax

```
wc [flags] filelist
```

Argument or Option	Description
filelist	A space separated list of file names of which to count the contents. If left blank, the standard output is read.

Flags

Argument or Option	Description
-c	Counts only the number of characters.

Argument or Option	Description
-w	Counts only the number of words. Words are any string of characters separated by a space, tab, or newline.
-l	Counts only the number of lines. Or, more precisely, it counts the number of newline characters encountered.

Note

Any combination of the flags in the list may be used. The default is all of them. When more than one option is specified, the output is in this order: lines, words, characters.

Message

```
wc: can't open filename
```

You invoked wc asking it to count in a file that it can't open. Either the file doesn't exit, or you don't have permissions to read it.

Examples

```
wc letter-to-dad
```

Tells you how many lines, words, and characters letter-to-dad is.

```
dd if=/dev/rct0 ¦ wc -c
```

Counts the number of characters found on the tape. In other words, it tells you how much data went on the tape. (It also is a useful way of validating that the tape is readable.)

what

Searches files for the occurrence of the character sequence
@(#), and prints the characters following until a ~, >, <, \,
null, or newline is found. The file name is shown followed
by a colon, and on the subsequent lines the string between
@(#) and terminator is also shown. what is intended to be
used by get in the SCCS system (source code control system).

Syntax

    what *filelist*

Argument or Option	Description
filelist	A space separated list of files to search.

Example

    what my-file

This looks at the file my-file and, if it finds the sequence
@(#), reports those lines.

who

Reports who is currently on the system and other user and
login information.

Syntax

    who [*flags*] *utmp-like-file*

    who am i

Argument or Option	Description
utmp-like-file	This is an alternative file to read to obtain login information. This is usually /etc/wtmp. /etc/wtmp is a history of what is found in the /etc/utmp file, and as it grows larger, it must be cleaned up periodically.

Flags

Argument or Option	Description	
-u	Reports those users who are currently logged on to the system. The following columns are reported:	
	NAME	The name of the user.
	LINE	The terminal they are logged on to.
	TIME	When they logged on.
	IDLE	The number of minutes since they've typed something in at their terminal. A period (.) indicates there has been some activity in the last minute.
	PID	The process-id of the login shell.
	COMMENTS	The comment field as defined in /tcb/files /inittab.

(continues)

Argument or Option	Description
-T	Indicates whether the terminal allows users to send messages to it. A plus sign (+) just before the LINE column indicates the terminal may be written to. A minus sign (-) indicates it cannot be written to, and a question mark (?) may indicate a problem with the terminal.
-l	Shows only those lines waiting for someone to log in.
-H	Prints the header line.
-q	Shows a space separated list of user names and a count; a quick version of the output. All other options are ignored.
-d	Shows the processes that have expired and have not been respawned by init.
-t	Shows when the system date/time last changed. It shows the old and new values.
-a	Shows all the information available.
-s	This is the default and limits the output to a form like -u, but only the following columns are provided: NAME, LINE, and TIME.

Examples

    who

Gives the columns: NAME, LINE, and TIME.

    who -t

Shows when the system time was changed.

See also

ps, whodo

whodo

Identifies who is on the system and what they are currently doing.

Syntax

whodo

whodo produces a merged output from the ps and who commands.

Examples

whodo

Produces a listing of who is on the system and what that user is doing.

See also

ps, who

write

Communicates with a user interactively, who is otherwise inaccessible.

Syntax

write *user tty*

Argument or Option	Description
user	The user name of the person to whom you wish to send a message.
tty	When the user is logged on to more than one terminal at a time, you may specify the terminal to which you want the message to go.

Note

write reads from standard input and each time you press Enter it sends that line to the user. When you press the end-of-file key (Ctrl-d) write exits.

Messages

```
Message from sending-user sending-tty
```

Means someone is writing to you. write lets you know who is sending the message and from what terminal they are running write.

```
(end of message)
```

The user sending you a message is finished.

```
user is not logged on.
```

You tried to write to a user who is not currently on the system.

```
permission denied
```

The user you want to write to doesn't want to be written to right now. The user most likely issued the mesg n command.

Tip

When you have finished a line of thought and want the person with whom you are communicating to respond, it is common practice to use the notation (o) to signal "over" and when you are finished with the conversation (oo) to signal "over and out." Multiple newlines also are used. Press the Enter key at least twice to signal the other user it is turn.

Tip

If the user has a phone, it is probably just as easy to pick up your phone and call. write is very useful when the phone isn't available, but it can be quite cumbersome because you can't begin your response until the other user completes a line of thought.

Novice users tend to get frustrated if they are written to because they are not comfortable enough with the system to respond. This is usually because they believe that the writing is messing up the application they are currently running, and some applications available on UNIX don't provide a redraw or shell escape function. This, in essence, cripples that user, even though no real damage has taken place.

Caution

If a user is logged on to more than one terminal, write assumes the terminal with the most recent login. This may not actually be the terminal he or she is currently on. Now you have to track down what the current terminal is; it may appear as though the user isn't able to respond. This problem is due to the multiple consoles and screen capabilities of UNIX.

See also

mesg, mail

xtod

Converts UNIX text files to DOS text files. UNIX uses one character to mean the end of a line: the newline or linefeed character. DOS uses two: a linefeed and a carriage return. Furthermore, DOS has an end-of-file marker (Ctrl-Z). If you do not convert the files, DOS will not like the files you create. Don't use xtod on binary/data files.

Syntax

    xtod *unix-filename*

Argument or Option	Description
unix-filename	The name of the UNIX file you want to convert to DOS format. If left blank, xtod reads from standard input. xtod always writes to standard output.

Example

    xtod letter-to-mom >dosletter

This converts the file letter-to-mom, and places the results into a file called dosletter.

See also

    dtox, doscp

yes

Continuously outputs the given string or the letter *y*. You can use this command when you run programs that require a yes response to prompts, but you can't be there to answer them.

Syntax

```
yes string
```

Argument or Option	Description
string	The string to continually output. If left blank, string generates the letter y.

Rule

yes continues to output the given string until it is aborted/killed. If it is in a pipe, it terminates when the program it pipes to terminates.

Example

```
yes ¦ rm my-file
```

If my-file does not allow for write permissions the rm command prompts for a yes or no response. This command shows the yes response. This duplicates the -f option to rm.

zcat

See compress.

Appendix

Regular Expressions

Regular expression is a term used in UNIX to describe pattern matching; regular expressions go beyond the simple notion of a wild card. Many of the UNIX commands use regular expressions (for example, grep, egrep, more, pg, ed, and so on). Regular expressions use a building block approach to pattern matching. The foundation of a regular expression is the *one-character expression*. One-character expressions are combined with other special characters to make regular expressions.

One-Character Expressions

One-character expressions match one character; thus their name. The following are valid one-character expressions:

.   Matches all characters in the position specified, except the new-line character.

[set]   Matches any character in the set. A set may be a list of characters or a range. A range is specified with a dash (-).

[0-9]   Matches the digits

[a-z]   Matches lowercase letters

> **Note**
>
> Remember that the set notation matches a single character. Futhermore the notation [0-9], matches digits, that is, the characters zero through nine, not numbers. In other words [10-20] would match either a 1, 0 through 2, or a 0, not ten through twenty, because 10 through 20 are values not digits.

If one of the characters you are looking for is the dash or the right square bracket they must be first in the set.

[-12]	Matches the characters - 1 2
[]12]	Matches the characters] 1 2
[]12-]	Matches the characters [1 2 -
[-]]	Matches the character -, followed by a]

In the preceding four examples the first three each returned any one character that matched any of the characters between the brackets. Because the fourth only has the dash "between" the brackets, this expression is looking for two characters, a dash followed by a right square bracket (-]).

Sets may be negated by using the caret (^) as the first character in the set:

[^-12]	Matches all characters except - 1 2
[^]12]	Matches all characters except] 1 2
[^]12-]	Matches all characters except [1 2 -

You do not have to escape other special characters such as ., *, [, and \. They are no longer special when used in set notation.

Any character is a one-character expression that matches itself, with the exception of the special characters:

```
.      *      [      \      ^      $      /
```

These special characters may be used to match themselves if they are preceded by a backslash (\). For example:

a	Matches the letter *a*
+	Matches the plus sign
\.	Matches the dot

Notice how the characters a and + didn't need to be escaped with backslash, but because the . is special, it did.

The Rules of Juxtaposition

Regular expressions are built from one-character expressions by *juxtaposition*. That is one-character expressions are placed next to each other to create a regular expression. For example:

[0-9].\$C	Matches any digits between 0 and 9, followed by any character at all, followed by the dollar sign, followed by an uppercase C.
abc123	Matches the letter a, followed by the letter b, followed by the letter c, followed by the digit one, followed by the digit two, followed by the digit three.

Note how the order in which the expression is written determines what it is going to match.

Enhancing One-Character Expressions

One-character expressions may have behavior modifiers that change how the one-character expression matches. The following table illustrates behavior modifiers.

Item	Description
*	If a one-character expression is followed by a star, then the one-character expression matches zero or more occurrences of that one-character expression.
.*	Matches no characters or any number of characters.
9*	Matches 9, 99, 999, *no nines*, 99999, and so on.
\\{*m*\\}	If this follows a one-character expression, then that one-character expression matches exactly *m* occurrences of that one-character expression.
.\\{2\\}	Matches two of any character.
a\\{8\\}	Matches eight letter *a*(s) in a row.
[0-9]\\{6\\}	Matches any six digits in a row.
\\{*m*,\\}	Matches at least *m* occurrences of the preceding one-character expression. There can be more, but there can't be less than *m* occurrences.
\\{*m*,*n*\\}	Matches at least *m* occurrences, but not more than *n* occurrences.
\\(*expr*\\)	Used as a placeholder, and is useless without the notation *n*. Each instance of the notation \\(*expr*\\) acts as a method of grouping regular expressions to be referenced later. *expr* is any valid regular expression.
n	Used to reference instances of the \\(*expr*\\) notation. It allows you to specify that you want to match the *n*th instance of \\(*expr*\\) at this point. The concept is best explained using an example. The password file has the form of:

```
user:encrypted_passwd:uid:gid:comment:home_dir:shell.
```

Item	Description
	We can use a regular expression to report all the users who's *uid* and the *gid* are the same number using grep. For example:
	`grep ".*:.*:\(.*\):\1:.*"` /etc/passwd
	This example looks for any number of characters, followed by a colon, followed by any number of characters, followed by a colon, followed by the "place holder" of any number of characters, followed by a colon, followed by the same pattern as found by the first "place holder," followed by a colon, followed by any number of characters. This prints a line every time the same number is used in the uid as the gid. A sample result may be:
	root:lakdfjl:0:0:root user:/:/bin/sh uucp:NOLOGIN:4:4:uucp user:/tmp:/bin/sh
^	The caret at the beginning of a regular expression *anchors* the regular expression to match at the beginning of the line.
	^a Matches any line starting with the letter *a*
	^[0-9] Matches any line starting with a digit
$	The dollar sign at the end of a regular expression *anchors* the regular expression to match at the end of the line.
	a$ Matches any line ending with the letter *a*
	[0-9]$ Matches any line ending in a digit

Note

The use of the caret (^) and the dollar sign ($) together means that the line exactly matches.

`^my big house$`   Matches any line with only the words "my big house" in it.

`^1$`   Matches any line with only the number one in it.

Index